INTEGRATE YOUR SHADOW

AND UNLEASH YOUR SUPERCONSCIOUS POWER

CHRISTOPHER M. DUNCAN

DUNCAN
PUBLISHING

Christopher Michael Duncan c/- Duncan Publishing
www.christophermduncan.com

Ordering Information:
Quantity sales. Special discounts are available on quantity purchases by corporations, associations, and others. For details, contact the "Special Sales Department" at the address above.

Integrate Your Shadow and Unleash Your Superconscious Power / Christopher Michael Duncan. –1st ed.
ISBN 978-0-9756139-0-0 (paperback)
ISBN 978-0-9756139-2-4 (digital)

INTRODUCTION

Like most people who pick up this book, you probably have a vision of what your life should look like, but maybe things aren't working quite the way you want, and you're ready for a transformation. Well, I have good news. What you learn here is some of the most advanced consciousness education you will find because it's about understanding yourself, your shadow, and your superpower. My wish is to set you free, so I hope you're excited about the change that's coming. The only way to embark on the journey we're about to go on together is with the end result in mind. So let's start there.

The two questions on your mind might be about who you are and what life is about. In my opinion, you, me, and every other human being are the same. We're all individual parts of one collective, creative consciousness. Each of us came into this world to have an individual experience of who we really are, and what we're open to learning and experiencing during our life as a human. We have only a limited time on this earth, so we need to make it count.

After working with thousands of people around the world in my Magnetic Mind program, I can tell you with total confidence that this thing we call a life and what makes it a good one comes down to one simple thing: how you feel about it. Yes, it really is that simple. Think about all of the times you've made drastic changes in your life. It all started with the knowledge that you didn't feel the way you desired to. For instance, realizing you're unhappy and unfulfilled in your relationship or that your job no longer challenges and uplifts you.

The only reason you want transformation is that, like most people I work with, you desire to change the way you feel. It's not really about money, healing, a new relationship, getting a new car, or a home by the beach. It's how those things make you feel. Just sit with that for a moment.

So why is it that you feel there's something missing? Why are you frustrated with your achievements, even if and when you're successful? Why is it that as soon as you get ahead, something happens that knocks you right back to where you started?

The core issue is that right at the start of your human experience, you learned a painful truth that wounded you, and as a result, you became stuck in a particular way of living, thinking, and being. This didn't happen for bad reasons, like being broke, but because your unconscious wants you to survive. The truth is, you're not broken, and you never were. In fact, you and everyone else have a superpower gained directly from the wounding experience.

I'm happy and fulfilled now, but I didn't always feel this way. I achieved success, but it was like there was a part of me that was fighting it. Nothing was easy, and I know I'm not alone in having that experience. In fact, if you're reading this book, you're most likely going through it right now, and you're looking for a better way. In the following chapters, I'll be exploring why many people struggle and what to do about it.

Most of us live in the shadow of our full potential, but imagine being the fully lit, bright flame that's your truest essence, instead of living in the shadow of it. You know there's something bigger out there for you, and every now and then you touch a spark of your true nature and purpose without being able to fully access it. And so you live a mere fraction of the life you could be. I want you to become whole, understanding how to unleash your superconscious superpower and integrate your shadow to finally receive and create to your fullest potential.

You've been living small due to the same fear that exists inside every one of us. But through the process, I will teach you, you'll become "unstuck," able to integrate your shadow and come out on the other side thriving. You'll be able to step into your full power and access the incredible gift of your superconscious superpower.

This book is written as a follow-up to my novel, *The Superconscious Path*, where I used the story of psychologist Michael Dunne to illustrate how it's possible to use and implement the superconscious creation process to shift from living an unconscious life to being in the magic of the superconscious path.

Here, I take those same learnings, messages, wisdom, and revelations, and present them in a way that further clarifies who you truly are and the ancient wisdom of the Enneagram, all in a way that's easy to understand and work with.

On my website, https://christophermduncan.com/books/, I provide resources that will enable you to integrate your shadow and activate your full superconscious superpower. If you want to get the most out of this book, there are free additional trainings, such as meditation and video sessions that will help you create your new life. I would recommend you log in and access the training portal now, so you have what you need to get the most out of this book.

The wisdom contained here changed everything for me, and it can do the same for you, too. You'll gain an understanding of your psyche, your behavior patterns, and the amazing potential that lies within you. Finally, the life you dream of and strive for can be yours.

My first book expressed the concept that you're not broken. Now, I'm taking you to another level, which is that your broken identity is actually your superpower. On the other side of your greatest fear, worry, or wound is a powerful genius that, once activated, will allow you to literally create magic. I'm so excited to take you on this journey with me. To support you, and so you get the most out of this book, I've created a free three-hour workshop and meditations to accompany it. Here's the link (https://christophermduncan.com/books/) to set yourself up with access to the workshop and meditations, so you're fully prepared for when you need it.

I so appreciate you, and I sincerely hope you follow the superconscious path to your new life. It's time to begin!

YOUR JOURNEY OF SELF-DISCOVERY BEGINS HERE

When you seek to understand yourself and grow as a person, you need to first look inside and examine who you truly are. If you can comprehend not only your own, but everyone else's, motivations, fears, and potential, you can achieve deeper connections and compassion with others you come in contact with, whether it's loved ones or strangers. That alone has the potential to make the world a kinder, more connected place for all of us.

The key to understanding all of this is the Enneagram, an ancient system that looks at personality types not as fixed characters, but as dynamic fluctuations within a specific orientation. In simpler terms, we each have a personality type; but within that personality type, there exists a variety of different behaviors that at any one time you're able to exhibit within the range of possibilities.

This is about more than just discovering who you are. It's about unveiling who you can become and reaping the benefits.

SELF-KNOWLEDGE

Socrates asserted, "The unexamined life is not worth living." To live a life of purpose and meaning, you must begin with self-examination. The nine orientational types offer a way of gaining insight into your core being, as well as your innate strengths and weaknesses.

It can be said that a weakness is simply a strength taken too far, and the path of integration shows how your intuition can fall from the highest to the lowest point of destruction. Recognizing the dangers inherent in your way of interacting with others will empower you to live your most authentic self.

UNDERSTANDING YOUR SHADOW

Without understanding the wound you carry and acting to neutralize it, you're destined to live in the shadow of your true potential. Your shadow is borne of your deepest fears, insecurities, and assumptions, all of which influence your thoughts, beliefs, and behavior, preventing you from moving forward.

PERSONAL GROWTH AND TRANSFORMATION

It's not just about learning, it's about doing. Putting what you discover into action so you grow as a person and truly transform your life. The ancient knowledge of the Enneagram, combined with the additional insights and teaching I'm providing, will help you step out from your shadow and embrace your true power as a superconscious creator. Once you have access to your superconscious superpower, you'll have a clear path to achieving your heart's desire.

SUPERCHARGE YOUR RELATIONSHIPS

Having a better understanding of yourself and others will foster healthier relationships, promote harmony, and achieve deeper connections. You'll learn how to relate to people authentically, communicate effectively, and handle conflict with compassion, which means less drama and more joy in your life.

ACHIEVE YOUR HIGHEST POTENTIAL

Imagine living your life with your intuitive powers fully realized, where you're empowered to embrace your strengths and recognize and mitigate old patterns of behavior when they show up. No longer in thrall to your fears, you'll become the most authentic version of yourself, living a life of purpose, wonder, meaning, and fulfillment.

CHAPTER 1

MY STORY

THE START

"I can't believe it happened again," I said to myself, my head in my hands hiding the tears welling up in my eyes.

I'd just had my third big business failure in under two years, I was over a million dollars in debt, and I had no idea how I was going to solve my problems.

There was a running tape in my head that sounded something like this:

- *How could I be so stupid?*
- *How could I end up in this mess again?*
- *Three business failures in fifteen months. Maybe I'm not cut out for this?*
- *I should just head home and get a job.*

Really, I didn't feel like I had any options.

Later that week my wife Harriet and I packed our bags, loaded our dogs into the car, and drove away from our home in Austin, Texas. Our destination was Harriet's family in England, and I got on that plane feeling like a total failure.

Just sixteen months earlier, I'd been on a roll. My business partner, Mark Deason, and I were flying high. "Deas" and I had grown our team to over forty staff and were making millions of dollars. I was a sought-after speaker and had been traveling the world teaching others how to set up their online businesses. I was engaged to the love of my life, and we'd moved to the United States to set up our new home.

How did I fall so far, so fast? In March of 2016, Deas was killed in a motorcycle accident, so on top of the personal devastation, my business fell apart, and I couldn't deliver on the promises we'd made. Not only that, but we'd been spending lots of money while not making much of a profit. Without Deas, I couldn't deliver, and I had no money to refund people. Not wanting his family to suffer or find myself in bankruptcy, I rang every creditor and client, clearly in a state of high emotion and emotionally broken. I put them on payment plans, figuring this was the right thing to do, postponed my marriage, and focused solely on ensuring the business didn't fall over.

In desperation, I created a business relationship with someone who promised they could fill Deas's role and went full force on ensuring I made at least $100,000 a month to pay all of my bills while starting the new business partnership. However, it turned out he couldn't deliver, and the pressure of the huge payments meant after one year, that business wasn't profitable. The partnership dissolved, and I was in an even worse position.

Somehow, I found another business partner who flew me to Texas, paid for six months on a rental property for us, and brought me on as a partner to do all of his marketing internally. Within two months, just as I was about to sign on, I realized his business was losing over $60,000 a month.

No thank you!

When I told him I couldn't be a partner, he dramatically locked me out of the business and told me that if I wasn't going to join him fully, he wouldn't pay me any of the profits I'd generated, and I now owed him for the property rental expenses!

It was all too much.

THE UNDERSTANDING

On that plane trip back to the UK, I couldn't sleep. Instead, I wrote out every failure and analyzed my journal to try and figure out what I was doing that had created this mess. My honest, unvarnished look at myself gave me enormous clarity, and I felt I was on the cusp of a big breakthrough.

In my bag stuffed under the seat in front of me, I had three books. One was on the unconscious identity structure, the second was about the Enneagram, and the last was about the spiritual practices of the ninja. What happened next can only be described as a miracle. I read each book cover to cover, the words nearly lifting off the page. Everything was so relevant.

Afterward, I began sketching out a framework, an understanding of the unconscious identity that relates to our personality, and I realized something as I connected this back to my situation: every failure I'd created reminded me of my childhood, and each was quite predictable.

As I reflected on every failed business scenario, I realized my partner was always a man in his forties, with similar personalities. They all doubted themselves, and instead of achieving their own vision, they used me to live their dreams. On the other hand, I was doing the opposite. Instead of going for my own vision, I gave my power to these people as a coach or mentor and was living their dream. This dysfunctional pattern of cocreation was exactly the same way I'd always related to my father.

THE EPIPHANY

A light bulb went off in my head. It was quite remarkable to see the truth written out on the page, staring at me. I'd been recreating the same pattern over and over again. My next rational thought was, *Maybe if I can figure out that pattern, I can stop repeating it.*

As I wrote out my failures in detail, the relationship became even clearer. It actually wasn't about my father at all. It had to do with how my consciousness was oriented. This knowledge brought relief that maybe the previous year of ups and downs hadn't been in vain. Maybe all of my actions were due to my unconscious wound causing me to repeat actions that had recreated all of this chaos in my life. It was like there were invisible structures forcing me into failure over and over again.

I sat back in my seat and let it all sink in. And as I did, I brought to mind the superconscious training I'd been going through over the last six months. So I closed my eyes and went through a process I will share with you in the following chapters that allowed me to understand what my unconscious was doing that was causing my repeating pattern of self-sabotage.

I realized what I'd been doing all my life was implementing a compensating strategy to avoid a wound or pain being true. This wound felt deep and ancient like it had been there my whole life. I felt ripped open and raw. It was obvious that who I believed myself to be was only a fraction of my truth, and I'd been denying a huge part of myself. As I started to realize this, a surge of energy swirled through me, and I asked myself some tough questions.

- Have I been living a fake life?
- Am I deceiving myself?
- Is it possible that even with all of the personal development and self-help I've done, I'm still denying who I really am?

The obvious answer was *yes*!

All the self-sabotage I was creating was because of one thing–my unconscious identity. It had been so focused on not allowing a wound to be accessed, it had sidetracked me into thinking that the whole point of life was to avoid this pain.

THE ORIGIN OF THE PAIN

What was the pain? Where did it come from?

I had no idea. All I knew was that this was the root of all of the dysfunction in my life, and in that moment, I chose to stop resisting the pain and just feel it. Tears streamed down my face. It hurt...and then it was over. Once I allowed myself to accept who I was and "died to the wound," everything changed. I was different in every way.

The man who got on that plane was not the same as the one who got off it! In just a few short hours, I'd decided to stop living from my childish worldview and accepted all that I was. During that transformation, I activated my full superconscious genius, and from that moment on, I stopped trying to fix myself, heal myself, or place any importance on being unique.

THE SUCCESS

Over the next three years, I built an eight-figure company, got married, and moved to paradise. I purchased homes and invested wisely, so I never have to work again. I wrote two books, one of them a *New York Times* bestseller, and transitioned into teaching others how to access their superconscious, recode their identity, and create a life they love.

The results have been phenomenal.

CHAPTER 2

YOUR TRUE NATURE

You're not just blood, flesh, and bone. You're a creative energy, a consciousness, having a human experience.

Let's presume that your consciousness has three distinct and separate memories or focuses, and each has a different purpose and objective.

1. The self-conscious

Your self-conscious, or thinking mind, decides what the ideal life looks like to you. It's logical and rational to want to achieve and enjoy the very best quality of life possible.

2. The unconscious

This is the part of you that's running your body, automatically performing all of the processes needed to keep you alive. It's fearful and emotional and has only one focus: surviving.

3. The superconscious

This is generally the most overlooked element of consciousness, the part of your mind that's filled with ideas, inspiration, and desire. It has no emotion, it's intuitive, and it has infinite wisdom and power. Its goal is to turn the invisible into the visible, to bring things into being, and to create.

In summary, the self-conscious chooses where you're going in life, the unconscious either allows it to happen or not, and the superconscious comes up with ways to turn the dream into reality. Your unconscious only wants to survive and learn how to do this at an early age. You're surviving now, and so as far as your unconscious is concerned, you're safe. It doesn't care how painful your life has been or is now This way of being is directly at odds with the self-conscious, which desires change and for you to thrive. It seeks excitement and fulfillment. And this polarity between the unconscious and the self-conscious creates all sorts of chaos in your life. The way it manifests is that as soon as you start winning or going for your highest goals in life, it's like an invisible hand pushes you into situations, decisions, and actions that lead you right back to where you started.

Remember my epiphany about how the misdirected focus of my unconscious led me to take actions that resulted in repeated failures? This is why you're constantly saying, "Here I go again!" and "Will I ever learn?" The conflict is created in your consciousness because you haven't yet integrated the wound of the unconscious.

YOUR TRUE SELF

You're a pure creative spirit, a superconscious being of nonform connected to everything through all time, space, dimensions, and reality. As a human being, you were born with a unique perspective, comprised of your body, your name, and the expression of your identity, which is a combination of your self-conscious and unconscious mind. And because you're a nonform, you have to learn how to operate in a three-dimensional reality or "world of form," orienting to the world through your limited vessel.

Your identity operates under an assumption that there's a "right" way to be, with a set of rules to understand, conform, or adhere to, while your consciousness wants to know "how it is." As a baby, you were driven to understand this, so your identity worked it out by seeking validation of its pure creative nature. Essentially, you needed nurturing and acknowledgment. You wanted to know if you had a heart and be assured that you could create through it and out into the world. What you learned was that you were just a vulnerable baby, dependent on the needs of others to survive.

This knowledge creates a wounding of feeling inadequate, an idea that's too painful and scary to be true. For example, no matter what you do, you don't receive validation for your accomplishments. Instead, you're told it's not good enough and where you can improve, so your deep-seated wound is "I am not enough," which makes you go for more, over and over again, to try and heal that wound.

Because this pain is unacceptable, you create a compensating or coping strategy that's experienced in two different minds. Your unconscious creates an agenda to never allow the pain to be true, and it does this by designing a life guaranteed to avoid pain. In contrast, your superconscious creates a superpower that accesses an intuitive wisdom to protect you. Interestingly, both parts are seeking the same resolution, which is to avoid the pain. However, they each take a drastically different approach to achieving that outcome.

HOW YOUR AGENDA IS CREATED

Pure Creative Energy

↓

Enters Vehicle Of Expression

↓

Desires To Know How It Is
(seeks to thrive and survive)

↓

Wounding Experience
(unmet needs)

↓

Create Compensating Strategy

↓

Creates Unconscious Agenda &
Superconscious Superpower

For example, a child living in an abusive household will learn that abusive people are unsafe. Once they survive the experience, the unconscious wants to ensure it can continue to survive, so over this person's lifetime, it will continue creating an acceptable amount of abuse and then find ways to escape from it. The learned pattern repeats itself over and over again to create safety and stay alive.

The superconscious facing this same wound creates awareness to identify liars, instinctively knowing who to trust and follow. This is your intuition. In my case, the wound was a deep feeling that I wasn't important or special. That I was broken and needed fixing. But this awareness was too painful to be true, and so I created a life to try and escape it. Of course, I was unable to do this, until I integrated this wound and accessed the superpower hidden within it, which changed everything,

THE UNCONSCIOUS AGENDA

Because the main objective of the unconscious is keeping you alive, it will continue seeking out the circumstances and life experiences it's already survived, even if they're painful. This is called the unconscious agenda. Put another way, the unconscious agenda is a pattern of behaviors and feelings your unconscious has learned is safe or survivable, and anything else is considered a threat.

In contrast, the self-conscious wants to thrive, creating the best, most fulfilling, and meaningful life possible, jam-packed with new experiences that are in complete opposition to the unconscious agenda. The conflicting agendas of the self-conscious and the unconscious cause great suffering because whenever you attempt to create your true desires, your natural creative ability gets overshadowed by your unconscious agenda. Just when you're gaining momentum, your unconscious will throw up a smoke-screen of thoughts and feelings that create a reality congruent with your wound. You then accept this as truth and do what you believe is needed to deal with that illusion. Essentially, you self-sabotage and end up with the same experience on a loop. And as much as you try to escape this cycle, nothing changes.

WHY DOES THIS HAPPEN?

The unconscious, knowing it can deal with the wound, doesn't want to get rid of it, while the self-conscious wants to change things for the better. The unconscious deals with this conflict by pretending it wants to escape the wound and focuses your thinking on how great it will be if you create your dreams, but in reality, it will never actually allow you to achieve them. It's quite happy with the wound and knows how to survive with the threat of the pain being true. If this sounds crazy to you, it is! But it's also the reality you face, meaning you won't actually change your life, even with all your good intentions.

This conflict leads to a life of oscillation, back and forth, like a pendulum. Lots of desire and action, but never really getting anywhere or maintaining whatever temporary change is achieved.

That said, it's not all bad because inside the wound, a superconscious superpower was created. Your specific superpower has remained dormant, waiting for you to let go of the unconscious agenda to awaken to it. And once that superpower is activated, you will be able to create with more ease, flow, and precision than you can truly imagine. Your superconscious is filled with so much wisdom, intuition, and genius that it will astound you.

THE WOUND AND THE SUPERPOWER

Since we're all different, with varied experiences in childhood and beyond, you're probably wondering if everyone has their own superpower. While, yes, we're all unique, there are just nine orientations we all fit into within the Enneagram system. Each orientation has a superpower and an unconscious agenda, borne from a specific wound with a specific lost childhood message, assumption, and a direct path to integration. But there's a way to let go of your unconscious agenda, integrate your shadow, and rise to live your superconscious superpower.

CHAPTER 3

YOUR LIFE FOCUS

There are effectively two ways to be focused in life:

1. Solving a problem
2. Creating a new reality

When you focus on solving a problem, you take action to make something go away, but focusing on creating means you try to make something come into being. By fixating on the problem, no matter how noble the idea of getting rid of it might be, you bring it into reality.

It's important to realize that you're not the problem. You're not broken, and you don't need to be fixed. The issue is the structure of the life you're living. Your focus creates your life structure, and that means it can be changed. Once you shift the structure, you'll flow easily toward success.

WHERE ARE YOU LIVING?

It's good to figure out where you're living. I don't mean geographically but where your attention is focused. Maybe it would be better to ask where you're creating your life from. Is it the past, the present, or the future?

I've worked with an incredible number of people, and they all seem to have one thing in common: a feeling that their "now" was lacking. They all believed that by striving to fix what was "wrong" with the present, they would be happier, wealthier, fitter, and stronger. In essence, their life would be much better

However, if you really desire to generate real change and achieve big results, you need to change the way you think now, and not waste energy focusing on your past and your problems or solving them and fixing yourself. Be in a creative-oriented life structure instead of a problem-oriented one, living completely in the present, with your focus directed toward your desired reality.

HOW TO CREATE YOUR LIFE STRUCTURE

I've talked about how we're all wrestling with internal conflict because the self-conscious wants the good life, the unconscious wants to survive, and the superconscious wants to make the dream a reality.

Take wealth, for instance. Most people desire more money, so they might do something like play the lottery to receive a life-changing sum of money and live the good life. However, most of the people who win the lottery lose it within three years, and believe it or not, are worse off than they were before. What happened? Well, this is the unconscious agenda in action, doing what it's supposed to do by keeping them "safe." While their self-conscious viewed these changes as good, the unconscious only wanted them to survive, which it did by keeping everything the same. And since "broke" was where they'd always been, that's where they were brought back to.

When your self-conscious takes action to move from the current reality to the desired reality, the unconscious will throw a spanner into the works and bring things back to where you've always been. The unconscious isn't being mean. It isn't the villain trying to ruin your life. On the contrary, it's trying to ensure your survival, and it knows you can withstand "how things have always been." The unconscious is narrowly focused on the fact that you survived your childhood wounds, so it seeks to recreate and outlive those experiences over and over again.

All of this results in an oscillating structure, moving back and forth, never getting anywhere. But you don't want to be stuck. You want to be in a flowing structure, gaining ground and making progress.

TENSION

How you structure your life makes all the difference because it creates tension, and tension creates movement. The law of tension is one of the most powerful laws in the universe.

When you generate tension in your life between what you have now and what you desire, you create an imbalance that needs to be resolved. The further away from the goal you are, the more tension you have, which is good because it's the magical force that will pull you toward your goal and what you desire.

FOCUS

Worrying about something puts you in a powerless structure where you can't create what you desire, but instead will only get more of what you want to avoid. Focus is the key to bringing about a flowing structure. Where you focus your attention is where all of your power rests. It moves your current reality toward your desired reality with ease.

The way you feel now must be how you feel in any future. That means you're not dependent on a specific outcome. You arrive at success or failure as the same person.

Remember, you're pure consciousness, creating everything you desire. You must be completely satisfied with "yourself" in the now and filled with your heart's desire to produce more of what you love. When you live from the creative orientation, you focus your attention on the end result and love the journey of getting there.

ACHIEVING FORWARD MOMENTUM

As you get in touch with your human experience, you might find you don't measure up in certain areas. And because you don't measure up, you let go of your true self, put on a mask, and focus on what you believe you're lacking.

And so instead of living your true self, you create a compensating strategy to fit in, proving to the world who you are by trying to fix something you perceive is wrong with you and thus be worthy of love. To be special and create peace, you give all of your power to this part of you and live from your shadow aspect, which is not your truth. In essence, you stop being that creative spark.

What happens is that you build your life around solving this problem, stuck in oscillation, because you're not actually being your true, authentic self. Most adults never live to the fullest expression of themselves. When you meet with people, what you're witnessing is their compensating strategy. Who they consciously and unconsciously believe they need to be to fit into society.

To achieve forward momentum and lasting change, you need to get out of that oscillating structure because that's where the problem lies. As I said, your structure comes from your focus, so to shift your attention, you need to neutralize the wound and integrate it back into wholeness.

You either live with psychological tension, trying to escape the wound, or in a desired reality with creative tension pulling what you desire into existence. You can't live in both structures. You're either creating magic or trying to avoid your wound being true.

Your superpower lies dormant, waiting for you to integrate the wound and activate it. Until you do this, you're just living in the shadow of your true self. You might have glimpses of your wholeness and feel it well up inside in those moments when you fully access your greatness, but most of the time, your life is just a shadow of what's possible.

First, you need to understand the wound. This will allow you to integrate the lost childhood message and access your superpower. You do this through the Enneagram.

CHAPTER 4

THE ENNEAGRAM

The Enneagram is an ancient Sufi teaching that describes nine unconscious orientations and their interrelationships, which affect how you see yourself and others It allows you to unlock your self-knowledge and activate your highest potential.

The Enneagram offers profound insights into the complexities of human nature. It not only helps you understand yourself but also provides a lens through which you can come to know the people around you.

The nine unconscious orientations are as follows:

1. The Perfectionist
2. The Helper
3. The Achiever
4. The Romantic
5. The Investigator
6. The Loyalist
7. The Enthusiast
8. The Protector
9. The Peacemaker.

THE ENNEAGRAM

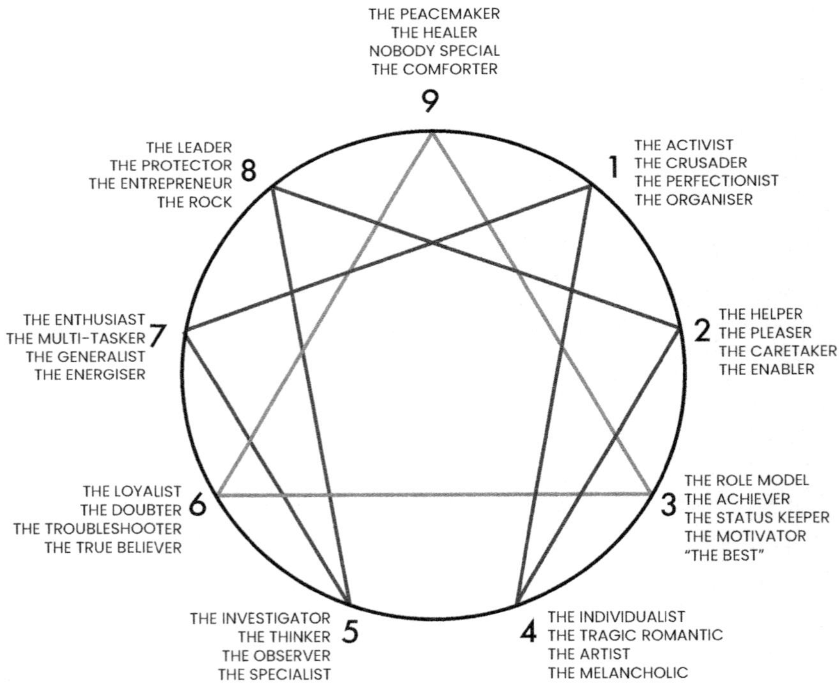

YOUR SUPERCONSCIOUS SUPERPOWER

Most teachers and students of the Enneagram have missed out on an essential element that got lost when it was brought forward. The Sufi teaching described all nine different fixations and their interrelationships. It explained the orientation points and how we get caught in them. What was not explained was that each orientation point is both powerful and destructive, with a superpower and a supervillain. Everyone has a base in one of the nine unconscious fixtures, that when accessed consciously on all levels, allows you to create complete magic here on earth. In other words, your consciousness creates everything.

You're now aware that we all live in two minds, one directed by your conscious thought and one directed by your unconscious agenda. Anytime the unconscious feels its survival is threatened, it creates a wound. To become a powerful creator and walk the superconscious path, you must know and understand your integrated personality type and how you orient yourself in the world. Only then can you use your superconscious superpower to create magic.

I'm going to do a deep dive into understanding the Enneagram to help you gain a full understanding of each personality type. Then I will share with you a powerful superconscious reset process, that will allow you to quickly integrate your wound and make the shift into accessing your superpower.

It won't matter if you've never seen or heard of the Enneagram before, as I'll be going through each orientation point in detail, expanding on the original teachings to give you the fullest appreciation of what it means to live from each orientation.

THE PATH OF INTEGRATION

Whichever Enneagram type you fall into, you can be in a dysfunctional, functional, or genius structure. The path of integration spans from less intuitive awareness to highly intuitive awareness, depending on how much you're caught in the unconscious agenda and wound. The more of your shadow you integrate, the higher you move up the path, toward integrated consciousness.

When in a dysfunctional state, intuitive power can become skewed and problematic, in the functional state, you can struggle with the balancing act of your intuition, while in the genius state, you're deeply attuned to your intuitive strengths. Let's take a closer look.

DYSFUNCTIONAL

This is the unhealthiest state. Here, the intuitive power of each type is distorted. For instance, Type 2s, the Helpers, often become overly focused on fulfilling others' needs and, in doing so, lose touch with their own intuition.

FUNCTIONAL

In the functional state, you often wrestle with your intuitive strengths, either overemphasizing or doubting them. For instance, Type 6s, the Loyalists, oscillate between sensing genuine threats and overreacting to perceived dangers.

GENIUS

In the genius state, you deeply attune to your intuitive strengths. This is the healthy end of the continuum. Here, each type's intuition operates at its peak. For instance, Type 4s, the Romantics, have a strong intuitive grasp of authenticity, allowing them to fully express their uniqueness and creativity.

UNDERSTANDING THE NINE TYPES

In the chapters that follow, I'll explore each Enneagram type to help you discover the intuitive strengths that define them, and examine the shadows that cloak those gifts. I'll trace the path of integration, from the lows of dysfunction to the pinnacle of genius, so you can understand what caused the wound and what it takes to heal it. Then you'll be able to activate your superconscious superpower and achieve your fullest potential.

Sometimes, it can be difficult to identify which orientational type is your main one, so I've added a set of questions at the end of each chapter that allows you to discover which type resonates with you, your feelings, and your lived experience.

If you get to the end of the book and are still uncertain about your unconscious agenda, the easiest way to understand it is to have a superconscious intuition session with a coach on my team. If you would like a one-to-one session, go to my website for more information.

The reason you need to understand your orientation point is so you can awaken your superpower, which is the intuition that transforms mere gut feelings and hunches into a profound understanding of yourself, others, and the world.

This book isn't just a tool for self-improvement. It's your guide to becoming the best version of yourself, an invitation to go on an extraordinary voyage of self-discovery and personal growth, where you'll unravel the mysteries of your own psyche and ascend to your highest potential.

CHAPTER 5

TYPE 1: THE PERFECTIONIST

"I HAVE A MISSION IN LIFE."

Type 1s, known as the Perfectionists, are predominantly guided by an inner quest for morality, decency, honesty, and integrity. They possess a well-defined moral compass that steers them through the ethical considerations of life. At their best, Type 1s exemplify high principles and conscientiousness, and hold themselves and others to the uppermost standards of ethical conduct, excellence, and precision. They usually have a clear understanding of what constitutes right and wrong, and invest significant effort into bringing about positive change in the world. But they can get caught up in striving to control what happens in regard to themselves and the world around them.

At the heart of the Type 1 personality lies a profound yearning for moral and ethical perfection, a drive that stems from the belief they will only be accepted, loved, and worthy if they meet impossibly high standards.

The other side of the coin is their core fear, which centers on anxiety relating to making mistakes or being fundamentally flawed. They're terrified of being perceived as morally imperfect or wrong, which often gives rise to an unrelenting internal critic, one that constantly evaluates and passes judgment on not only their actions but also on those around them. This self-critical disposition has a big impact on their self-esteem and self-worth, which turns into a driving force for self-improvement and becomes the foundation for their internal turmoil.

KEY CHARACTERISTICS AND TRAITS

1. Perfectionism

Type 1s are renowned for their pursuit of perfection, setting lofty standards for themselves and anticipating a similar level of excellence from others. They have a desire for meticulous attention to detail and can become disheartened when outcomes fail to meet their rigorous standards.

2. Strong morality and ethics

They possess a strong commitment to what they perceive as moral and ethical ideals and are unyielding in abiding by their moral code. Frequently, they emerge as advocates for justice and social transformation, enthusiastically working toward fixing perceived imperfections in the world.

3. Hypercritical

Type 1s possess a relentless inner critic that consistently assesses their actions, which generates stress and imposes a sense of guilt when they believe they've fallen short of their self-imposed high expectations.

4. Highly structured and organized

They're drawn toward organization and methodical planning, preferring a structured routine to ensure everything aligns in perfect order.

5. Anger-prone

Under stress, Type 1s may grapple with pent-up anger and frustration, which occasionally manifests as a violent outburst or passive-aggressive conduct.

6. Intense desire for improvement

Type 1s are driven by a profound yearning for self-improvement and personal growth. They're invariably motivated to improve both themselves and the world around them.

7. Elevated sense of responsibility

Type 1s often shoulder a substantial burden of responsibility, and they can become weighed down by their compulsion to fix issues they perceive as wrong, damaged, or broken, whether in their own lives or in the broader world.

PERSONALITY PROFILE

- Self-righteous
- Judgmental and critical
- Need to be seen as perfect.
- In a constant battle between "how it is" and "how it should be."
- Strongly reject their dark side.
- Difficulty allowing themselves to have negative emotions, to the point they lose their importance.

Type 1s desire to live in an "ideal" world. They've been known to leave a life of security and comfort to pursue what they believe is a higher calling so they can improve the lives of others or the world at large. They represent a characteristic that seeks the feelings of being a "good girl" or "good boy." This part of themselves learned to behave properly, take on responsibility, and most of all, be correct in the eyes of others. Because this part remembers being painfully criticized, they learned to monitor themselves severely, to avoid making mistakes that would come to other people's attention.

Type 1s embrace the belief that by being strict with themselves in the pursuit of perfection, they will gain justification in the eyes of the world, but often the result is a kind of personal misery. Their inner critic gains control, and it can be hard to break free from it.

They're usually unaware that they deny themselves pleasure. They're so preoccupied with what they "should" do and what they "must" do, that they rarely ask themselves what they want to get out of life. Their natural wishes were forbidden when they were young, and so they learned to block out their desires by focusing attention on what's correct.

HOW TYPE IS MANIPULATE

Perfectionists often manipulate situations and relationships by imposing their high standards on others, believing that their way is the right way. They will criticize, correct, and "instruct" people to get them to comply with their requirements, and if their advice is resisted, they can become angry.

BASIC FEAR

The primary fear of Type 1s is making mistakes and/or being flawed. They fear being defective, evil, or corrupt.

BASIC DESIRE

Their fundamental desire is to be good, morally right, virtuous, and to have integrity.

THE EGO MESSAGE / MAIN UNCONSCIOUS MESSAGE

Think of Type 1s as bearers of an invisible standard emblazoned with the message, "You're only okay if you're perfect." It shapes the lens through which they view themselves and the world around them, basically reinforcing their belief that it's not okay to make mistakes. This concealed message, buried deep within their psyche, drives a ceaseless pursuit of perfection and a longing to conform to their own and society's standards, as well as a compulsion to improve or correct everything they encounter.

In childhood, they established a pattern of behavior whereby they tried to be good kids. They often report feeling that they needed to justify their existence because simply being a child wasn't enough. As a result, many young Type 1s think being a child is an imperfect state, and so they seek to take on adult roles and adopt a serious outlook at an early age. They understand their parents need a lot from them, and they can play the role of the family hero.

Type 1s often experience a disconnection from their protective figure. The result is a feeling that they must parent themselves. They can become diligent and strict, choosing to set high standards for themselves, establish their own moral guidance system, and self-police their own behavior. They will go to great lengths in detriment to their own happiness and become a prisoner of their own rules and definitions.

LOST CHILDHOOD MESSAGE

You're good, and you're loved just as you are.

Type 1s were raised in an environment where mistakes weren't tolerated, thus fueling their pursuit of perfection.

UNPACKING THE UNCONSCIOUS MESSAGE

Let's take a look at what their unconscious message translates to.

Perfection as a condition of being worthy

Type 1s often grow up feeling that their inherent worth is contingent upon their ability to be faultless. They internalize the idea that any deviation from perfection is a direct reflection of their inadequacy.

Relentless self-criticism

The need to be perfect fuels their internal critic, a relentless voice that constantly evaluates and scrutinizes their actions and the actions of others. Any perceived shortcomings are met with self-judgment and the belief that they've fallen short of being "good" or "okay."

Constant striving for moral excellence

To reconcile their belief in perfection, Type 1s dedicate themselves to upholding the highest moral and ethical standards. They strive to be virtuous and to correct any perceived wrongs in themselves and in the world around them.

Anxiety and stress

The burden of consistently seeking perfection can lead to significant stress and anxiety. Type 1s may find it challenging to relax or accept imperfections in themselves, others, or their surroundings.

ASSUMPTION

Type 1s assume that they must maintain perfection to lead a meaningful life, earn the respect of others, and create what they want.

COMPENSATING STRATEGY

Type 1s often compensate for their inner critic by striving for perfection and seeking to control their environment. They will avoid doing tasks, unless they can be done perfectly, believing that by adhering to strict principles, they can eliminate imperfections and find a sense of peace. When necessary, they will be defensive or deflect criticism of something or someone else.

GIFT

Type 1s are powerfully motivated to be honest, to walk the walk, be consistent, and act with integrity.

They can see the good/perfection in everything, know how to do things right, and possess great wisdom regarding moral values. They care deeply about being good people and are inspired to solve world problems.

HOW THIS ORIENTATION WAKES UP TO THEIR POWER

Type 1s regain their power by embracing self-compassion and acknowledging that they're lovable and worthy, flaws and all. This transformation involves letting go of the need for constant correction and cultivating self-acceptance.

SUPERCONSCIOUS SUPERPOWER / INTUITION STYLE

Impeccable moral compass

Type 1 individuals possess an intuitive understanding of the moral order in the world. They can instantly recognize ethical choices, making them reliable judges of right and wrong.

Injustice detector

Type 1s have incredible intuitive powers, enabling them to detect even the subtlest injustices. They can identify areas where fairness is compromised, intuitively guiding them toward rectifying these issues.

High standards of excellence

Type 1s have an intuitive grasp of what excellence looks like. Their inner compass helps them set high standards for themselves and those around them.

Navigating with Intuition:

Type 1s frequently rely on their intuition for decision-making and problem-solving, guided by their resolute moral compass. Their intuition acts as a navigational instrument, directing them along the path of righteousness and moral integrity.

PATH OF INTEGRATION (FROM DYSFUNCTION TO GENIUS)

As I said, the path of integration spans from less intuitive awareness to high intuitive awareness, as influenced by how much someone is still caught in the unconscious agenda and wound. The more you integrate your shadow, the higher you move up the path. Let's take a closer look at what that means for a Type 1.

DYSFUNCTIONAL

Level 1: Violation

At this stage, Type 1s can become self-righteous and authoritarian. They fear their ideals may be wrong, which is possible, but they're unable to admit it. To cover up their insecurities, they seek to justify themselves, at times acting out their inner frustrations in destructive ways, being closed-minded, and allowing no compromises or negotiations on their positions, as this would mean admitting they're not perfect. These actions cause harm to themselves, as well as everyone around them.

Level 2: Obsession and compulsion

The Type 1's perfectionism becomes obsessive, fostering compulsive behavior and mental distress. They act out their repressed desires while publicly continuing to condemn them, which distorts and weakens their core self, making them out of control.

Level 3: Pathological destructiveness

In the unhealthiest stage, driven by an unrelenting pursuit of an unattainable ideal, Type 1s become incapable of supporting themselves or the people and world around them. They realize they've lost control of themselves and are doing the very things they won't tolerate. In trying to rid themselves of their obsession, they may become destructive, both to themselves and others.

FUNCTIONAL

Level 1: Imbalance / social role

In this stage, they begin to fear that others are indifferent to their principles. They become serious and driven, often disapproving, controlling, and inflexible in their moral judgments, which creates relational imbalances.

Level 2: Interpersonal control

Type 1s fear condemnation for any deviation from their ideals, and can become excessively critical of both themselves and others. To control and correct, they stifle their own growth and potentially the growth of everyone around them.

Level 3: Overcompensation

They may become fanatical about perfection, obsessing over rules and regulations. Fearing others will spoil the order and life balance they've achieved, they get angry that their ideals aren't taken seriously, which ultimately leads to isolation. Consumed by detail, they neglect the bigger picture.

GENIUS

Level 1: Liberation

At their healthiest, Type 1s are able to relinquish rigid perfectionism and approach life without reacting to it emotionally. They foster self-acceptance and extend the same to others, utilizing their desire for improvement to enhance the world. As a result of their self-actualization, they achieve wisdom and discernment.

Level 2: Psychological capacity

At this level, Type 1s have emotional resilience, adapting gracefully to life's imperfections, while seeking to be sensible, moderate, and objective.

Level 3: Social value

Type 1s command immense respect for their integrity. They're ethical and self-disciplined, and possess a strong sense of purpose and conviction, putting aside personal desires for the greater good. Their commitment to bettering the world garners recognition and admiration.

HOW TO HEAL THE WOUND

Healing the wound of a Type 1 involves a journey of self-discovery, self-acceptance, and self-compassion, eventually realizing that making mistakes is an entirely normal and acceptable element of human existence.

Type 1s would benefit from

- making peace with their internal critic and accepting all parts of themselves, others, and the world around them without judgment;
- accepting and allowing people, themselves included, just to be who they are; and
- acknowledging the truth on their own, in their own time.

Healing happens when they understand that acceptance doesn't reduce the capacity to be discerning, choose wisely, or act with integrity. It removes rigid structures that can make life uncomfortable for themselves and the people around them.

FAMOUS EXAMPLES OF PERFECTIONISTS

Mahatma Gandhi

Gandhi's life was an embodiment of the Type 1 personality. His unwavering dedication to nonviolence and quest for social justice and transformation, epitomize their relentless pursuit of moral ideals. He's revered in India as the father of the country.

Angela Merkel

As the first female Chancellor of Germany, serving between 2005 and 2021, Merkel characterized in her leadership Type 1's strong sense of responsibility and moral integrity. She governed her political realm deftly and enjoyed enormous popularity and confidence. During her chancellorship, she was considered to be the most powerful woman in the world.

Michelle Obama

The former First Lady of the United States embodies the essence of a Type 1 through her commitment to education, health, and social justice. Her initiatives and advocacy for positive change reflect her inner drive to improve life for all people. She's still highly influential. In 2020, for the third year running, she topped the Gallup poll of the most admired woman in America.

Florence Nightingale

The pioneer of modern nursing tirelessly pursued perfection in healthcare, leaving an indelible mark on the profession. Her constant dedication to improving hygiene and nursing standards led to the extension of patients' lives. She founded a school of nursing to pass on her knowledge and practices, which established the basis of healthcare as we know it.

IN SUMMARY

Understanding Enneagram Type 1, the Perfectionist, offers a journey into the realm of high standards and steadfast moral integrity. These individuals strive for perfection in a world teeming with imperfections, thus fostering inner conflict and complex relationships. By gaining an understanding of hidden and lost messages, and the compensatory strategies they employ, Type 1s may embark on a path of self-discovery and healing.

To identify a Type 1, search for their dedication to perfection, resolute moral principles, and ceaseless pursuit of improvement.

TEN QUESTIONS TO UNCOVER TYPE 1 TRAITS

1. Do you often establish demanding standards and strive for perfection in your professional and personal life?
2. Are you inclined to criticize both yourself and others, driven by a robust sense of moral integrity?
3. Do you wrestle with accepting imperfections in yourself and the world around you?
4. Are you predisposed to institute rules and structure in your life and the lives of others?
5. Does your dedication to bettering the world drive your actions and ideals?
6. Do you grapple with self-criticism and an unceasing fear of making mistakes?
7. Have you received feedback indicating that you're excessively critical or judgmental?
8. Do you find yourself gravitating toward roles laden with responsibility and leadership?

9. Are the guiding forces of your life your moral principles and the quest for virtuous conduct?
10. Have you encountered difficulty relinquishing your need for control and perfectionism?

CHAPTER 6

TYPE 2: THE HELPER

"I CAN MAKE ANYONE LIKE ME."

Type 2s are known as The Helpers due to their perpetual desire to assist, care for, and uplift those around them. Their primary motivation is to be loved and valued, genuinely believing that by providing these services to others, they can gain the love and appreciation they crave.

At their best, Type 2s are nurturing, selfless, and exceptionally empathetic, genuinely concerned about the well-being of others, and always ready to provide assistance without expecting anything in return. But the downside of their altruism is that they often have huge difficulty acknowledging their own pain and needs, and are drawn to automatically see it in others. On some level, they're trying to fix the hurt that they're unable to acknowledge and fix in themselves.

At the heart of the Type 2 personality lies a profound belief that they're only truly loved and valued when they're indispensable. They've learned that they can't express their needs directly, and so they hope others will pick up hints and act on them to repay the Type 2 for their service. They're really bad at receiving money and payment for their help and have a strongly judgmental ego that directs what they believe they must do to be loved, as well as what counts as love. For a Type 2, having needs and striving for goals is selfish and bad.

KEY CHARACTERISTICS AND TRAITS

1. Helpfulness

Type 2s are well-known for their eagerness to assist and support others. They readily offer their help and often go to great lengths to fulfill the needs of those they care for.

2. Desire for love and acceptance

Their core desire is to receive love and acceptance from others. They often believe that the path to securing this love is through being indispensable and helpful.

3. Extreme empathy

Type 2s possess a high degree of empathy, allowing them to intuitively understand the emotional needs of those around them and respond with care and compassion.

4. Self-neglect

In their pursuit of being helpful and appreciated, Type 2s might overlook their own needs and well-being, sometimes to the point of exhaustion.

5. Fear of rejection

They grapple with a deep fear of rejection or being perceived as unnecessary. This can lead them to be overly accommodating and prone to people-pleasing.

6. Conflict aversion

Type 2s have a tendency to avoid conflicts and disagreements to maintain harmony in their relationships.

7. Boundary challenges

Setting and maintaining healthy boundaries can be a struggle for Type 2s, often causing them to overextend themselves and experience resentment as a result.

PERSONALITY PROFILE

- Sociable
- Behave how they assume others want them to
- Don't know their own mind
- Manipulative
- Stoic
- Unable to recognize the difference between their own wishes and complying with or fighting against what other people want.

As children, Type 2s earned love and security by adapting their feelings to suit the concerns and needs of others, in an attempt to ensure their own popularity. If they fail, the adapting habit can become compulsive to the point where they forget their own needs and even their true personality.

Because they've suppressed their own desires in the interest of pleasing everyone else, Type 2s tend to become indispensable to their partner or to people in power as a way of getting those forgotten needs met. If results fail to materialize, there's a good deal of complaining because the balance between giving and getting didn't even out

Beneath the surface, Type 2s feel worthless and mask this by presenting a false image of being completely generous and unselfish, not wanting any payoff for themselves, when in fact they have enormous expectations and unacknowledged emotional needs. Often, after they have helped someone who then moves on, they're left with heartbreak and resentment.

As they outgrow their search for approval, they develop an exquisite personal radar for the detection of moods and preferences.

HOW TYPE 2S MANIPULATE

Type 2s may manipulate through giving and caring, which is sometimes done with unacknowledged strings attached. They might expect appreciation or reciprocity for their assistance and feel hurt if it's not acknowledged. Their manipulation can be subtle, such as asking for something without letting the other person know they're owed for their kindness and are not above guilt-tripping.

BASIC FEAR

The Type 2 core fear is that they won't be needed, loved, or wanted, and end up alone.

BASIC DESIRE

The Type 2's fundamental desire is to feel loved and valued, acknowledged and cherished.

UNCONSCIOUS EGO MESSAGE / MAIN UNCONSCIOUS MESSAGE

Type 2s carry an unconscious message that tells them, "You're only valuable when you're needed." This message drives their persistent desire to be indispensable and can lead to feelings of emptiness when they perceive themselves as unnecessary.

The learned childhood pattern is that to function within the family system, you need to be the helper, the selfless friend, the pleaser, and the giver of attention to everyone else. Type 2s have three rules:

1. Put other people's needs ahead of your own.
2. Give to get.
3. You must earn affection because love isn't given freely.

Type 2s believe it's selfish to acknowledge their own needs, and so they repress them and attend to everyone else's first. Their dysfunctional structure concludes that sacrificing themselves for others is the richest way to live and also the only way they can be loved.

Feeling less important than everyone else drives their compulsion to put others first, lavishing attention on them in the hope they'll be needed and liked because they're only okay if they're close to and liked by everyone.

LOST CHILDHOOD MESSAGE

Your needs are just as important as everyone else's.

Type 2s were raised in an environment where they felt insignificant, thus compelling them to seek validation and love by fulfilling the needs of those around them.

UNPACKING THE UNCONSCIOUS MESSAGE

Let's take a look at what their unconscious message translates to.

Constant giving

Type 2s prioritize helping and supporting others at the expense of their own needs.

Approval-seeking

Type 2s seek external validation and affirmation as a way to confirm their value, going to great lengths to ensure they're indispensable to maintain a sense of being loved and valued.

Fear of rejection

The fear of being rejected or deemed unnecessary is a core concern, so they avoid abandonment or criticism at all costs.

Suppression of needs

Type 2s often suppress their own needs and desires, sometimes even neglecting self-care, in the pursuit of being needed and loved.

ASSUMPTION

Deep within their psyche, Type 2s assume they must fulfill the needs of others to be loved and accepted. It's as if they believe their role is to be the selfless, caring, and nurturing friend, partner, or family member.

They become the martyr, and it's only when they perceive they've done enough for others that they go for what they want.

COMPENSATING STRATEGY

Type 2s often compensate for their fear of being unloved by becoming the ultimate caregivers, constantly anticipating and meeting the needs of others. They focus on being a supportive person, helping, and putting every first. This selflessness is often at the expense of their own well-being.

GIFT

Type 2s make good things happen for people. They will stay up late to take care of children or elders, travel across town to provide food, or see to it that the people they care about get medical treatment. When there's practical work to be done, healthy Type 2s will be there.

The gift of their sincere, supportive works speaks more eloquently for them than anything they could say. Thus, Type 2s are gifted with the extraordinary ability to go beyond the simple means of caring for people and create something truly meaningful.

HOW THIS ORIENTATION WAKES UP TO THEIR POWER

The journey to empowerment for Type 2s is to recognize the importance of self-care and setting healthy boundaries. Once they do, they can become even more effective caregivers.

SUPERCONSCIOUS SUPERPOWER / INTUITION STYLE

Empathetic antennae

Type 2s have intuitive radar for perceiving the needs and desires of those around them. They can sense when someone requires support or attention, often offering help before it's requested.

Emotional insights

Intuition guides them to read between the lines of people's emotions. They can pick up on unspoken feelings and offer comfort or assistance accordingly.

Relationship harmonizers

Type 2s possess intuitive skills for maintaining harmonious relationships. They can sense when conflicts are brewing and work to mediate and bring people back together.

PATH OF INTEGRATION (FROM DYSFUNCTIONAL TO GENIUS)

DYSFUNCTIONAL

Level 1: Violation

At this stage, Type 2s fear they're driving people away, which may be true, so they'll try to elicit pity as a substitute for love, keeping others dependent on them to prevent them from leaving. They can become intrusive, controlling, suffocating, and emotionally volatile, and will rationalize their behavior by seeing others as "selfish."

Level 2: Obsession and compulsion

Type 2s could become so desperate for love that they pursue it obsessively. Struggling with feelings of inadequacy or jealousy, their care is offered with a sense of urgency. They feel they're entitled to whatever they want because they've suffered so much, which makes them act out their need for affection recklessly and inappropriately.

Level 3: Pathological destructiveness

In the unhealthiest stage, driven by a desperate need for validation, Type 2s can be destructive, both to themselves and others. Their care can become toxic and harmful. The realization that they may have been "selfish" or harmed others is too much, so they fall apart, physically and emotionally, playing out the role of victim and martyr, which requires people to step in and take care of them.

FUNCTIONAL

Level 1: Imbalance / social role

In this stage, they may begin to fear that whatever they've been doing isn't enough, and others don't really want them around. In seeking reassurance, they can become overly giving, pleasing, and flattering people to gain approval or validation. Their care can feel smothering, the abundance of attention, stifling.

Level 2: Interpersonal control

Type 2s worry that the people they love will love someone else more, so they'll put the needs and wants of others first while struggling to express their own needs and desires. Their assistance can take on a manipulative quality, making it difficult for them to thrive independently.

Level 3: Overcompensation

They may overextend themselves and feel unappreciated, angry that others are taking them for granted, but unable to freely express their hurt. This can lead to resentment, their care offered grudgingly, as they exhaust themselves, unable to enjoy the process of helping or the outcome achieved. Repressed feelings begin to cause physical problems.

GENIUS

Level 1: Liberation

At their healthiest, Type 2s let go of the belief that they're not allowed to care for themselves and learn to prioritize self-care and set boundaries. They provide support without losing themselves in the process and recognize themselves for their genuine care and empathy, thus becoming joyous, gracious, and humble.

Level 2: Psychological capacity

Well-adjusted Type 2s focus on the feelings of others with loving concern. They develop emotional resilience and a sense of self-worth, allowing them to function in a way that supports everyone, including themselves, and become loving, thoughtful, and selfless.

Level 3: Social value

Self-assured Type 2s are cherished for their genuine care and compassion. They reinforce their self-image by doing good deeds, they're generous with their time and energy, and are appreciative, encouraging, and supportive. They're also emotionally expressive and enjoy sharing their talents.

HOW TO HEAL THE WOUND

Healing the wound of a Type 2 involves a process of self-compassion and learning to prioritize their own needs, recognizing that their worth isn't solely defined by their ability to help others.

Type 2s would benefit from

- understanding it's impossible to heal your heart through self-sacrifice;
- appreciating that real love isn't scarce, nor is it a commodity that can be won; and
- knowing the only person who can love you deeply, consistently, and under all circumstances, is yourself.

Type 2s must turn inward to connect and look after themselves with the same level of love, compassion, and care they provide to others. It's imperative for them to listen to their own needs and create strong boundaries to ensure they maintain their energy levels.

FAMOUS EXAMPLES OF HELPERS

Princess Diana

The Princess of Wales was known for her warmth, empathy, and tireless work for charitable causes. Her ability to connect with people on a deeply emotional level, as well as her desire to make a positive impact, reflects the best qualities of a Type 2. She's especially known for her acceptance and support of AIDS sufferers at a time when they were often ostracized.

Dolly Parton

Born into poverty, musician Dolly Parton has used her wealth to support many charitable endeavors. Her father never learned to read or write, which led her to establish Dolly Parton's Imagination Library, which posts a book every month, from birth to kindergarten to each enrolled child, equating to around 850,000 children.

Steve Buscemi

Successful actor Steve Buscemi supports many charities that seek to make life better for people, including Action Against Hunger and Friends of Firefighters. He was a New York City firefighter from 1980 to 1984, and he turned up at his old firehouse to volunteer the day after the September 11 attacks, working twelve-hour shifts alongside the regular firefighters.

Florence Henderson

The actress, best known for her role as Carol Brady on *The Brady Bunch,* radiated warmth and maternal care. Her portrayal of a nurturing and supportive mother figure aligns with the Type 2's inclination to provide love and assistance.

IN SUMMARY

Understanding Enneagram Type 2, the Helper, allows us to navigate the complex landscape of a personality driven by an unceasing desire to care for others. They provide warmth, compassion, and support, but may sometimes struggle to express their own needs and desires. By gaining an understanding of hidden and lost messages, and the compensatory strategies they employ, Type 2s can embark on a path of self-compassion and self-care.

To identify a Type 2, observe their helpful and caring nature, emotional empathy, and longing to be appreciated for their nurturing spirit.

TEN QUESTIONS TO UNCOVER TYPE 2 TRAITS

1. Do you often go out of your way to help and care for others, even at the expense of your own needs?
2. Is your self-worth closely tied to your ability to assist and support those around you?

3. Do you feel uncomfortable expressing your own needs and desires, fearing it may burden others?
4. Have you been told that you're exceptionally nurturing and empathetic?
5. Does the idea of not being needed or appreciated cause you distress?
6. Are you prone to putting the well-being of others ahead of your own, sometimes to the point of self-neglect?
7. Have you ever felt unappreciated or hurt when your efforts to help weren't acknowledged?
8. Do you have a natural knack for understanding and empathizing with the emotional needs of others?
9. Is it difficult for you to say "no" when someone asks for your assistance, even when you're overwhelmed?
10. Do you often feel a strong desire to be loved and valued by everyone you encounter?

CHAPTER 7

TYPE 3: THE ACHIEVER

"IF I WORK HARD ENOUGH, I KNOW I CAN BE THE BEST."

Type 3s, the Achievers, are driven by a relentless pursuit of success, recognition, and excellence. They're primarily motivated by the desire to be seen as successful and to receive admiration and validation from others. They have a natural knack for setting and attaining goals and are often seen as ambitious, goal-orientated, and adaptable.

At their best, Type 3s are authentic, driven, ambitious, confident, and persistent. They take care of themselves physically, make it their business to learn about themselves and how to manage their affairs better, and are capable of achieving remarkable success in their chosen field.

Because they often rely on their intuition to gauge the expectations and desires of those around them, they possess a keen sense of what people admire and are skilled at adapting to meet those expectations. At the heart of the Type 3 personality lies a deep-seated belief that their worth is intrinsically tied to their achievements.

The other side of the coin is that they feel they're nobody and have no value without their achievements. In the rush to attain whatever they believe will make them more valuable, they can become so alienated from themselves that they no longer know what they really want.

By recognizing that their value isn't solely defined by their accomplishments, Type 3s can embark on a journey of self-discovery, embracing their authentic selves and finding a healthier balance in their relationships, and lives.

KEY CHARACTERISTICS AND TRAITS

1. Ambition

Type 3s are marked by their ambitious nature, constantly striving for personal and professional success. They set high goals and work tirelessly to attain them.

2. Desire for recognition

Their core desire is to receive recognition and admiration from others. External validation is a measure of their worth.

3. Adaptability

Type 3s are skilled at adapting to different situations and presenting themselves in a favorable light. They often possess strong interpersonal and communication skills.

4. Image consciousness

They're acutely aware of their image and how they're perceived, which can cause them to project a polished and idealized version of themselves to the world.

5. Fear of failure

Type 3s harbor a deep-seated fear of failure and rejection, which can drive them to avoid situations where they might not succeed or be celebrated.

6. Competitiveness

They're often highly competitive and strive to outperform everyone, whether in their careers or personal life.

7. Workaholic tendencies

In their pursuit of success, Type 3s may become workaholics, sometimes neglecting their own well-being or personal relationships.

PERSONALITY PROFILE

- Competitive
- Self-promoting
- Over-achieving
- Workaholic
- Perpetual student
- Identify strongly with achievement and success
- Undertake several endeavors at once
- Use activity as a form of control
- Veer from problems by introducing new projects
- Reframe failure into success
- Discredit sources of criticism

As children, Type 3s were prized for their achievements. Performance and image were rewarded rather than emotional connections, so they learned to suspend their own feelings and instead focus their attention on earning the status that would guarantee them love.

At an early age, they decided they couldn't have feelings and needed to be someone else to be accepted. It was important to avoid failure because only winners were worthy of love.

Type 3s are high achievers, identifying with the popular image of youth, energy, and competition. They're always finding ways to enhance and improve their own lives and teach others how to develop themselves.

They're chameleons who can tune into the valued successes of any groups they belong to, unwittingly believing that whatever image receives approval from those they respect, is the one they should adopt. These can range from an adorable child in a TV ad, a superhuman who gets the job done, a high-powered executive, or even someone who's completely laid-back.

As failure is to be avoided, Type 3s redefine it as a partial success or pin the blame on others. They feel a strong urge to escape a shaky project or sinking relationship and quickly move on to better things because their worth depends on what they do and what they achieve, rather than who they are.

A sense of inner optimism is often bolstered by paying selective attention to positive achievements. They tend to pursue what others reward and gradually lose touch with themselves. Inch by inch, their own heart's desire is left behind, until it's completely forgotten.

HOW TYPE 3S MANIPULATE

Type 3s might manipulate through their adaptability and image management. They can present themselves in a way that suits the desires of others, rather than expressing their true selves, employing a carefully crafted image to gain approval and validation.

BASIC FEAR

Their fundamental fear involves being perceived as a failure, worthless, and without value apart from their achievements.

BASIC DESIRE

Their fundamental desire is to feel worthwhile, accepted, and desirable, and to be seen as successful, admirable, and worthy of respect. They yearn for recognition.

UNCONSCIOUS EGO MESSAGE / MAIN UNCONSCIOUS MESSAGE

Type 3s carry an unconscious message etched into their psyche that tells them, "You're only worthy when you achieve and excel." This unspoken message fuels their unrelenting drive for success and can lead to an inner void when they perceive themselves as failing.

As children, Type 3s weren't valued for themselves. Instead, they were praised for performing extremely well in certain areas, which taught them to get a sense of self-worth through achievement and performance. However, this eventually proved unsatisfying because it was validation of what they'd done, not who they were.

They have a deep emotional bond with the nurturer of the family, yearning for this person to tell them, "You're wonderful, you're pleasing, and you're welcome in this world." Because they want to be validated, they learn to adapt themselves to do and be what's pleasing to that person, which usually takes the form of being the family hero.

The core message for a Type 3 is that they're okay and good, as long as they're successful and others think well of them, which causes them to believe that they must achieve to be loved and accepted. This drives their compulsion to succeed and gain awards, attention, and admiration.

LOST CHILDHOOD MESSAGE

You're loved no matter what you do.

Type 3s were raised in an environment where they were only recognized when they excelled, thus propelling them into a ceaseless quest for success and admiration. It's as if they were living on a stage where applause followed every accomplishment.

UNPACKING THE UNCONSCIOUS MESSAGE

Let's take a look at what their unconscious message translates to.

Pursuit of success

Type 3s internalize the notion that they're loved and valued when they excel and achieve. They often prioritize external success and recognition as a way to validate their self-worth.

Image and persona

They may create a polished image or persona that aligns with what they believe will garner approval and admiration, which can lead to a disconnection from their authentic selves.

Fear of failure

The fear of failure and inadequacy often looms large for Type 3s. They may go to great lengths to avoid any perception of falling short in the eyes of others.

Restlessness and perfectionism

Type 3s may exhibit restlessness and perfectionism, constantly striving for greater success and accolades. This drive can lead to burnout and a sense of emptiness.

ASSUMPTION

Deep within their psyche, Type 3s often assume they must present a flawless image to gain love and admiration. It's as if they're performing on a grand stage, where the audience expects nothing but perfection. They believe if they accomplish enough, they will be valid.

COMPENSATING STRATEGY

Type 3s seek to accomplish and learn, and often compensate for their fear of inadequacy by becoming expert chameleons. They adapt to the expectations of others and become who they need to be to have success, which allows them to excel in a variety of roles and settings.

GIFT

Type 3s help others be their best, using their ability to excite and motivate people to succeed more than they thought they could. For example, Type 3s who are nurses, doctors, teachers, or therapists, can act as a catalyst for their students and clients by the power of their own example.

Type 3s also use their talents and presentation skills to advance worthy causes. As a result, they often become outstanding role models in their fields of endeavor. They're good communicators and promoters, and they know how to present something in a way that's attractive, appealing, and inspiring. They can be highly effective at building morale and community spirit. Many corporations and organizations employ healthy Type 3s to represent them.

HOW THIS ORIENTATION WAKES UP TO THEIR POWER

The journey to empowerment for Type 3s is akin to a grand transformation, much like a caterpillar becoming a butterfly. By recognizing the value of authenticity, they can harness their drive for success to achieve their true desires, rather than chasing empty accolades. This metamorphosis frees them from being a performer and launches them as the genuine star of their own life.

SUPERCONSCIOUS SUPERPOWER / INTUITION STYLE

Success mapping

Type 3s have a remarkably uncanny ability to identify goals and what it takes to achieve them. They can effortlessly chart a course to success, seeing the steps and strategies needed.

Self-presentation

Type 3's intuition guides them to present themselves effectively, understanding how to adapt and showcase their best qualities in various situations.

Understanding market trends

Type 3s often possess an intuitive insight into market trends and consumer behaviors that enable them to make informed decisions about business and investments.

PATH OF INTEGRATION (FROM DYSFUNCTION TO GENIUS)

DYSFUNCTIONAL

Level 1: Violation

At this stage, Type 3s may rightly begin to fear they're failing, and their claims are empty and fraudulent. In such cases, they can become manipulative, deceitful, and ruthlessly competitive, pursuing success at any cost, and sometimes hurting people in the process. Internally, they feel empty and depressed.

Level 2: Obsession and compulsion

Their drive for success becomes obsessive and compulsive. Desperate for attention, they'll concoct any story or scheme to cover their decline, leading to a disregard for the well-being of themselves and others. They don't want anyone to know how troubled they are and will go to great lengths to keep their emotional illness and misdeeds hidden.

Level 3: Pathological destructiveness

In the unhealthiest stage, Type 3s can become self-destructive and harmful to others in their pursuit of success. If they feel there's nothing they can do to win the approval they seek, they might lose control of their repressed anger. Their achievements can be destructive and chaotic, and they'll seek revenge on whoever they feel has rejected them.

FUNCTIONAL

Level 1: Imbalance / social role

In this stage, Type 3s may begin to fear their accomplishments will be overshadowed by the successes of others. Driven by the need for external validation, they could become overly image-conscious, adapt to the expectations of others, and seek to distinguish themselves by over-achieving.

Level 2: Interpersonal control

Type 3s could begin to worry they will lose esteem. Ambitious but self-doubting, they want to be well-regarded and desired. They struggle to express their true desires and emotions, and become overly focused on achievement, trying to present what they believe is the best possible image. Their adaptability can lead to a lack of genuine connection.

Level 3: Overcompensation

Type 3s may become obsessed with success and recognition, to the detriment of their well-being and authenticity. They fear others won't notice them unless they're hugely successful, and so try selling the reality of their grandiose claims by being self-promoting, competitive, and arrogant. Their achievements may lack genuine fulfillment.

GENIUS

Level 1: Liberation

At their healthiest, Type 3s learn to embrace their authentic self, pursuing success for personal fulfillment rather than external recognition. They let go of the belief that their value is dependent on the positive regard of others and become admired for their inherent charisma and unique achievements. They're self-accepting, genuine, and benevolent.

Level 2: Psychological capacity

Type 3s cultivate self-awareness and emotional depth. They're attuned to what others value and adapt themselves to become someone who's more valuable. They can navigate their own, and other people's, emotions with authenticity and empathy. They seek to be capable and well-adjusted.

Level 3: Social value

Type 3s are recognized for their genuine achievements and magnetism. They reinforce their self-image by developing themselves and their talents and inspire others to pursue their true desires. They're competent, confident, and persistent, becoming exemplary in whatever they do.

HOW TO HEAL THE WOUND

Healing the wound of a Type 3 involves embracing their authentic self and recognizing that they're inherently worthy of love and admiration, regardless of their achievements.

Type 3s would benefit from

- letting go of the belief that their value is dependent on the positive regard of others
- having the courage to allow the mask to come off and feel the perceived emptiness inside
- seeing their authentic value without achieving something to feel valuable.

Type 3s need to understand that they're valuable just as they are, simply because they exist. When they're willing to risk losing the approval of others to follow their own heart, they're free to be the outstanding individual they always wanted to be.

FAMOUS EXAMPLES OF ACHIEVERS

Oprah Winfrey

The media mogul, philanthropist, and talk show host embodies the quintessential Type 3. Her journey from troubled childhood to becoming one of the most influential figures in media exemplifies their drive for success and recognition.

Steve Jobs

The cofounder of Apple Inc. and a visionary in the world of technology, Steve Jobs epitomized the Type 3's pursuit of excellence and innovation. His relentless drive to create groundbreaking products mirrors the Type 3's quest for success.

Serena Williams

The legendary tennis player has consistently pushed the boundaries of her sport. Her journey from humble beginnings to the pinnacle of success reflects the Type 3 unyielding pursuit of excellence.

IN SUMMARY

Understanding Enneagram Type 3, the Achiever, lets us into the complex world of individuals driven by an unceasing pursuit of success and recognition. They excel in various roles but sometimes grapple with authenticity and genuine connections. By gaining an understanding of hidden and lost messages, and the compensatory strategies they employ, they can embark on a path of self-discovery and fulfillment.

To identify a Type 3, observe their drive for success, adaptability, and longing for external recognition.

TEN QUESTIONS TO UNCOVER TYPE 3 TRAITS

1. Are you driven by a relentless pursuit of success and achievement in various areas of your life?
2. Is your self-worth closely tied to the recognition and admiration you receive from others for your accomplishments?
3. Do you find it challenging to express your true emotions and vulnerabilities to those around you?
4. Are you often viewed as confident, competent, and capable in your pursuits?
5. Have you ever felt a deep fear of failure and the accompanying loss of external validation?
6. Do you often adapt to the expectations and desires of others to achieve your goals?
7. Have you been told that you're highly ambitious and image-conscious?
8. Is it difficult for you to slow down and be content with your achievements without seeking the next big success?
9. Do you sometimes feel a sense of emptiness when external recognition and rewards are lacking in your life?
10. Do you feel a strong desire to be admired, recognized, and respected for your successes?

CHAPTER 8

TYPE 4: THE ROMANTIC

"NO ONE UNDERSTANDS ME BECAUSE I'M UNIQUE."

Type 4s, the Romantics, are marked by their deep connection to their emotions, unique sense of identity, and steadfast quest for authenticity. They possess an introspective disposition and a propensity for creative self-expression.

At their best, Type 4s are creative, emotionally attuned, and capable of inspiring others with their authenticity. They perceive themselves as distinct and cherish the emotional depth and richness of their inner world. Often relying on their intuition to understand and express their emotions and unique identity, they possess an innate sense of what feels authentic to them and may express this through creative endeavors. At the heart of the Type 4 personality lies a profound belief that their worth is inextricably tied to their uniqueness and individuality.

The other side of the coin is their deep fear of being perceived as ordinary, just like everyone else, and as such, worthless and uninteresting. Type 4s are primarily motivated by the desire to find their unique identity and to be authentic.

KEY CHARACTERISTICS AND TRAITS

1. Emotional depth

Type 4s are known for their profound connection to their emotions and often experience a wide range of intense feelings. They value truthfulness and self-expression.

2. Desire for individuality

Their core desire is to be seen as exceptional and special. They feel a sense of otherness and strive to stand out from the crowd.

3. Creativity

Type 4s frequently possess creative talents and an inclination toward artistic self-expression. They use creativity as a means to explore and communicate their complex inner world.

4. Emotional intensity

They could experience emotional highs and lows more acutely than other types, leading to a heightened sense of emotional turmoil and introspection.

5. Fear of being ordinary

Type 4s often have a deep fear of being ordinary or unimportant, which can drive them to pursue uniqueness and resist conformity.

6. Tendency toward self-absorption

In their quest for self-discovery and authenticity, Type 4s may sometimes become overly self-absorbed, focusing on their own feelings and experiences to the detriment of their relationships.

7. Longing and melancholy

They may grapple with feelings of longing and melancholy, desiring what they perceive as missing or unattainable in their lives.

RELATIONSHIP DYNAMICS

In relationships, Type 4s may seek deep emotional connections while also struggling with a fear of rejection, afraid they're too intense or different for others to understand or accept.

PERSONALITY PROFILE

- Insecure
- Melancholy
- Cool
- Stylish
- Artistic
- Depressed
- Trouble accepting loss, unable to mourn and set it aside
- Sensitive
- Easily hurt.
- Tendency toward hyperactivity.

Type 4s remember abandonment in childhood, and as a result, they suffer from a sense of deprivation and loss, and a subsequent lowering of self-esteem. There are three kinds, ranging from fundamentally depressed, fundamentally hyperactive, and primarily swinging in mood between these two extremes. But the one thing they have in common is that they all feel something vital in life has been taken away from them, and they're seeking to regain what was lost

Type 4s are hurt by social oversights and perceived slights, such as a missed birthday, so they'll make casual sarcastic remarks that can lead to alienation from their friends. Relationships are negatively affected by their habit of focusing attention on the negative aspects of whatever they're going through.

They base their identity on their internal feelings, which is a problem because they're always changing, and therefore their identity is always changing. Whatever their feelings are, they try to intensify them, so they can bolster their sense of self. They're always looking for the mother or father who ignored and/or belittled them.

Because they have doubts about their identity, they tend to play "hide and seek," hoping their absence will be noticed.

HOW TYPE 4S MANIPULATE

Type 4s might manipulate through their emotions, sometimes leveraging the depth of feeling to elicit sympathy or attention. For example, they might accentuate their sadness or sense of being different to gain recognition and understanding.

BASIC FEAR

Their core fear revolves around having no identity and no personal significance. They dread being overlooked and deemed insignificant.

BASIC DESIRE

In direct contrast to their fear, their primary desire is to be seen as authentic, unique, and irreplaceable. Type 4s yearn to express their true self, to find themselves and their significance, and to create an identity out of their inner experience.

UNCONSCIOUS EGO MESSAGE / MAIN UNCONSCIOUS MESSAGE

Type 4s carry an unconscious message that tells them, "You're only worthy when you're unique and authentic." This message propels their quest for individuality and can lead to feelings of inadequacy when they perceive themselves as ordinary, so they're constantly comparing themselves to others.

In childhood, they felt as if they weren't like their mother or father, and never fit in, almost as though they were switched at birth. They didn't feel "seen by" or sufficiently "connected to" at least one of their parents. Because of this, they came to believe there must be something profoundly wrong with them, which launched them on a lifelong search for self, seeking the answer to the question, "Who am I?"

They tend to focus on what they lack or what makes them different. In childhood, they felt abandoned and misunderstood by their parents and later in life by other significant people.

Type 4s can become unconsciously attached to experiencing problems and may be reluctant to let go of painful feelings because as children they learn to get attention from their family by having emotional issues. They feel they must get a grip on their negative emotions before they can do anything productive in life, believing they're only assured of people's love for them by being difficult and seeing if they respond.

Their core belief is that they're only good and okay if they're true to themselves., which drives their compulsion to express themselves creatively.

LOST CHILDHOOD MESSAGE

I see you and understand you.

Type 4s grew up in an environment where they were only praised for being special and unique, thus propelling them into a lifelong quest for individuality and self-expression.

UNPACKING THE UNCONSCIOUS MESSAGE

Let's take a look at what their unconscious message translates to.

Pursuit of individuality

Type 4s internalize the belief that they're loved and valued when they express their distinctive, authentic selves. They often seek to differentiate themselves from others, striving for originality.

Embracing emotional depth

They're naturally inclined to explore their deep emotions and uncommon inner experiences. This emotional depth often sets them apart and forms a crucial part of their identity.

Fear of being ordinary

Type 4s may have an intense fear of being ordinary or mundane. They tend to avoid conforming to societal norms and expectations, opting for a more offbeat, unconventional path.

Melancholy and longing

The pursuit of uniqueness can lead to feelings of melancholy and a sense of longing. Type 4s may feel that something is missing, or they're not living up to their own ideals.

ASSUMPTION

Deep within their psyche, Type 4s assume they must cultivate a significant identity that sets them apart from others to be loved and appreciated. It's as if they're the authors of their own life stories, constantly seeking to spin a compelling narrative.

All Type 4s were abandoned in childhood, either literally or effectively, and so assume there's something about them that makes them unlovable.

COMPENSATING STRATEGY

Type 4s often compensate for their fear of insignificance by developing a special identity and embracing their emotional depth. They aim to be attractive enough to be loved and to cover up or fix what's wrong with them. They become the curators of their inner world, expressing their feelings and individuality through various forms of self-expression, be that art, music, fashion, or personal style.

GIFT

Type 4s are able to communicate subtle truths about the human condition that are profound, beautiful, and affecting. Because they're attuned to their inner states, subconscious feelings, and impulses, they're usually highly intuitive, which feeds their self-discovery and creativity.

Although they may have intellectual gifts, Type 4s tend to rely on what their intuition is telling them about themselves and their environment from moment to moment. Often they're not sure how they arrive at their insights. They find the inner workings of their own consciousness mysterious and surprising.

HOW THIS ORIENTATION WAKES UP TO THEIR POWER

The journey to empowerment for Type 4s is akin to a phoenix rising from the ashes. By recognizing their inherent worth and the beauty in their identity, they can harness their creativity and depth of feeling to express their truth and inspire others. Think of an artist finding the courage to display their work in a gallery or participate in a poetry reading, unapologetically showcasing their individuality.

SUPERCONSCIOUS SUPERPOWER / INTUITION STYLE

Authenticity radar

Type 4s have a deep intuitive sense for recognizing authenticity. They can instantly perceive when something is genuine and when it lacks depth.

Creative expression

Type 4's intuition leads them toward creative endeavors. They can sense unusual avenues of self-expression and often produce original art, music, or literature.

Emotional depth

Type 4s innately navigate their own emotions, understanding their intricacies. They're in touch with their emotional landscapes and can often guide others through theirs.

PATH OF INTEGRATION (FROM DYSFUNCTION TO GENIUS)

DYSFUNCTIONAL

Level 1: Violation

At this stage, Type 4s may become melodramatic, emotionally volatile, and attention-seeking. They justly fear they're wasting their lives, so they use their emotions and uniqueness to manipulate others and reject whatever fails to support their self-image or emotional demands. Repressed feelings can result in depression, apathy, and constant fatigue.

Level 2: Obsession and compulsion

Their emotional intensity becomes obsessive and compulsive, leading to a disregard for the well-being of themselves and others. They loathe themselves and hate others for failing to save them. They may create drama and chaos to gain attention, thus sabotaging whatever good is left in their lives.

Level 3: Pathological destructiveness

In the unhealthiest stage, Type 4s can become hazardous and harmful to themselves and others. Believing they've wasted their lives pursuing futile fantasies, they resort to extreme measures in their pursuit of individuality and emotional intensity, often attempting to elicit rescue through self-destructive behavior.

FUNCTIONAL

Level 1: Imbalance / social role

In this stage, they may become overly focused on their emotional intensity and individuality, sometimes struggling with feelings of envy and believing they're misunderstood or undervalued. They fear that their changing feelings won't sustain them and their creativity, so they use fantasy and style to bolster their originality and dream of someone rescuing them.

Level 2: Interpersonal control

Type 4s can struggle to express their true emotions and identity, finding it difficult to connect with others on a deep level. As a test to figure out if people are really interested in them, they act aloof, self-conscious, and melancholy, believing their fragility will attract a rescuer and keep others away.

Level 3: Overcompensation

Type 4s fear they'll be forced to give up their dreams. They may become fixated on their unique identity, which causes isolation, melancholy, and emotional intensity, making them wallow in self-pity, despairing that they'll never be rescued. Feeling like they're missing out on life, they exempt themselves from "the rules," becoming sensual, pretentious, and unproductive

GENIUS

Level 1: Liberation

At their healthiest, Type 4s learn to embrace their true self and express their individuality without the need for external validation. They relinquish the belief that they're more flawed than everyone else, and so gain freedom from self-absorption. They become admired for their creativity and emotional depth, inspiring others to explore their own authenticity.

Level 2: Psychological capacity

Healthy Type 4s develop self-awareness and emotional depth, navigating their own emotions and those of others with genuineness and empathy. They focus on their own feelings and preferences to establish a clear sense of personal identity, acknowledging that they're sensitive and different.

Level 3: Social value

Well-adjusted Type 4s reinforce their self-image by expressing their individuality through innovative action. While their means of self-expression are highly personal, they often have universal implications. They're eloquent and subtle, recognized for their genuine creativity and emotional depth. They share their feelings, inspiring others to pursue their true desires and express their own identity.

HOW TO HEAL THE WOUND

Healing the wound of a Type 4 involves them recognizing their inherent worth and the uniqueness of their identity. They need to understand that they don't have to create drama or embrace suffering to be appreciated.

Type 4s would benefit from

- letting go of the idea they're more flawed than anyone else, believing they're as good as anyone else, and no one needs to rescue them;
- understanding that being unique and being true to one's self doesn't require effort;
- being grateful for their past suffering and pain because it's allowed them to become the person they are today;
- realizing the universe has only created one of them, meaning they're both exceptional and a part of everything else;

- knowing they're not isolated or alone; and
- allowing themselves to simply be, and use their intuition and creativity to make their impact on the world.

FAMOUS EXAMPLES OF ROMANTICS

Frida Kahlo

The renowned Mexican artist, Frida Kahlo, is a quintessential Type 4. Her paintings are a reflection of her deep emotional world and her quest for authenticity. She expressed her pain, passions, and individuality through her art, which continues to resonate with audiences worldwide.

Vincent van Gogh

The iconic Dutch painter, Vincent van Gogh, is renowned for his emotionally charged and distinctive artwork. His paintings, including *The Starry Night*, and the many and varied self-portraits he produced, showcase his originality and profound emotional connection to the world.

Kurt Cobain

The late Kurt Cobain, musician and frontman of Nirvana, epitomizes the Type 4's quest for realness and self-expression. His music and lyrics are marked by their emotional depth and a longing to march to the beat of his own drum.

IN SUMMARY

Understanding Enneagram Type 4, the Romantic, grants us access to a world of profound emotions, unique identities, and a dogged quest for authenticity. They excel in their capacity for emotional depth and creativity but sometimes struggle with feelings of longing and a need for recognition. By gaining an understanding of hidden and lost messages, and the compensatory strategies they employ, Type 4s are able to embark on a path of self-acceptance and self-expression.

To identify a Type 4, observe their depth of emotions, creativity, and longing for truthfulness.

TEN QUESTIONS TO UNCOVER TYPE 4 TRAITS

1. Do you constantly seek authenticity and individuality in various aspects of your life?
2. Is your self-worth closely tied to being recognized and appreciated for your unique identity and emotional depth?
3. Do you often struggle with a sense of longing or melancholy, yearning for something more meaningful or special?
4. Are you prone to expressing your emotions and individuality through creative outlets like art, music, or personal style?
5. Have you ever felt a deep fear of being ordinary and overlooked?

6. Do you frequently believe that you're different from others and that your emotions are more intense or profound?
7. Are you often seen as introspective and deeply in touch with your feelings?
8. Is it challenging for you to accept criticism or rejection, as it feels like a personal attack on your uniqueness?
9. Do you have a strong desire to be seen as authentic and emotionally genuine, even if it means experiencing intense emotions?
10. Have you ever felt a sense of emptiness or a void that you believe can only be filled by expressing your particular identity and emotional depth?

CHAPTER 9

TYPE 5: THE INVESTIGATOR

"IF I CAN UNDERSTAND IT, I'M SAFE."

Type 5s, the Investigators or Observers, are driven by a thirst for knowledge, a longing for privacy, and a compulsion to understand the world around them. They possess a deep need for understanding, information, and self-sufficiency.

At their best, Type 5s are insightful and innovative, capable of making a valuable contribution in a variety of situations thanks to the wealth of knowledge they've acquired and retained. They often rely on intuition to break down complex issues, gather information, and explore and assess concepts and theories, while also having the ability to see patterns and connections others might miss.

At the core of the Type 5 personality lies the profound belief that their needs and desires are unwanted and a burden. But the other side of the coin is that they're primarily motivated by the desire to acquire knowledge and maintain autonomy. They have a natural predisposition for analytical thinking and introspection and a preference for curbing their own needs.

KEY CHARACTERISTICS AND TRAITS

1. Intellectual curiosity

Type 5s are marked by their insatiable curiosity and keen desire to explore and understand the world. They may seek to acquire knowledge as a means of self-preservation.

2. Desire for independence

Their core desire is to maintain a sense of independence and self-sufficiency. They're often reluctant to depend on others or to feel intruded upon, preferring autonomy and privacy.

3. Analytical thinking

They possess a strong preference for analytical thinking and will work to understand complex ideas and systems in depth.

4. Minimalism

In a bid to conserve and maximize their mental and emotional resources, Type 5s may adopt a minimalist approach, limiting their personal needs and restricting interactions with others.

5. Fear of inadequacy

Type 5s harbor a deep fear of inadequacy or being unable to cope with the demands of life. This can compel them to accumulate knowledge and become outstanding experts in their chosen fields.

6. Tendency to withdraw

Type 5s may be inclined to withdraw from social situations and emotional entanglements, opting instead to direct their energy and attention toward intellectual pursuits.

7. Reluctance to share knowledge

Having gathered knowledge and information, and gained insights, Type 5s might be reluctant to share what they've learned, making open collaboration difficult.

RELATIONSHIP DYNAMICS

In relationships, they may struggle to open up emotionally, as they don't find it easy or natural to share their innermost thoughts and feelings.

PERSONALITY PROFILE

- Self-sufficient
- Aloof and detached
- Focused on acquiring knowledge.
- Reluctant to share
- Prefers to work alone
- Values privacy and solitude.
- Denies or restricts their own needs.

Type 5s are exceptionally private people. They like to live in secluded places, away from social demands and emotional stress, because they felt intruded upon as children and denied the privacy they craved. Their strategic defense is withdrawal by minimizing contact, simplifying their needs, and doing whatever they can to protect their private space.

They believe that harboring desires and intense emotions indicates a lack of control and that painful feelings should be ignored. They feel a sense of achievement in being able to easily detach from the needs that dominate other people's lives. To control a situation, they'll simply stop reacting to it, rather than trying to take charge, making them appear lonely and socially isolated, but solitude is their preference.

They pursue knowledge relentlessly, due to deep insecurities about their ability to function in the world, and generally don't believe they have the ability to do things as well as others. Consequently, they tend to avoid dealing with their more practical problems, instead focusing intently on mastering one key area to feel competent. And once they become the expert in that area, they don't require social validation. The irony is that no matter how competent they become on a subject, they're unable to resolve their biggest insecurities in life.

HOW TYPE 5S MANIPULATE

Type 5s can manipulate through their detachment and emotional withdrawal, using their independence and knowledge to create distance and maintain control in their relationships. They may also withhold information or emotional intimacy to protect themselves.

BASIC FEAR

Their core fear revolves around the dread of being helpless, incapable, incompetent, or overwhelmed.

BASIC DESIRE

Their primary desire is to be self-sufficient, knowledgeable, and capable. They yearn to navigate the world independently and contribute their wisdom.

UNCONSCIOUS EGO MESSAGE / MAIN UNCONSCIOUS MESSAGE

Type 5s carry an unconscious message that tells them, "You're only worthy when you're self-sufficient and knowledgeable." This propels their pursuit of understanding and autonomy, and can lead to feelings of inadequacy, should they see themselves as uninformed or dependent.

In childhood, they didn't feel safe in their family and looked for other ways to feel confident and secure. They established a pattern where they retreated into their own private place to escape and then turned their attention away from personal and emotional needs to something objective. Essentially, they cut themselves off from painful feelings by staying in their minds.

They're the least materialistic and don't need anything. Their motto is, "I won't ask anything of you, so you don't need to ask anything of me." They're happier alone and expect little other than to be allowed to pursue their own interests unimpeded by any demands, needs, or emotional problems. In this way, they can feel safe and in control of their lives. They develop a mastery of different subjects, so they have something to bring to the table when they do feel ready to connect with others.

The belief that drives their compulsion to need nothing and know everything in their chosen field, is that they're good and okay only if they've mastered something.

LOST CHILDHOOD MESSAGE

It's okay to ask for help.

Type 5s were raised in an environment where they had to be self-sufficient and gather knowledge to be valued, which translated to them as, "Your needs are intrusive and unwelcome," thus propelling them into a lifelong quest for understanding and independence.

UNPACKING THE UNCONSCIOUS MESSAGE

Let's take a look at what their unconscious message translates to.

Withdrawal and independence

Type 5s withdraw from others and seek independence. They often strive to be self-reliant and self-sufficient, believing it's the only way to avoid saddling people with their problems.

Pursuit of knowledge

To mitigate being unwelcome, Type 5s often turn to intellectual pursuits, gathering knowledge and expertise to limit their reliance on others.

Minimalism and privacy

They may adopt minimalist lifestyles, keeping their needs and personal space as unobtrusive as possible. Privacy is highly valued, as it allows them to avoid feeling like a burden.

Emotional reserve

Type 5s might hold back their emotions, as expressing needs and feelings can be seen as intrusive or vulnerable.

ASSUMPTION

Type 5s often assume they must gather knowledge and be self-sufficient to be loved and appreciated. They fear that if they open their boundaries, their private space will be invaded and destroyed.

COMPENSATING STRATEGY

Type 5s often compensate for their fear of inadequacy by seeking autonomy and immersing themselves in intellectual pursuits. They withdraw, remain aloof, and protect themselves by living cerebrally. They become researchers of their own minds, striving to understand both their field of interest and their inner selves.

GIFT

The main gifts a Type 5 brings to the world involve their tremendous insights and understanding, coupled with their areas of expertise. This allows healthy Type 5s to understand many points of view at the same time, so they can comprehend both the whole and its component parts. Their ability to entertain different perspectives without being attached to any of them makes them excellent arbitrators and problem-solvers.

Type 5s are extraordinarily observant and perceptive. They're sensitive to their environment and perceive subtle changes or discrepancies that others might miss. This is because they have one or more of their senses developed to an unusual degree. Some might have high visual acuity with regard to color, while others are tuned into sounds, easily recognizing rhythms and pitches.

Type 5s never lose their childhood curiosity or take anything for granted. If they want to know what's under a rock, they get a tool, dig out the rock, and take a good look.

Type 5s also possess an extraordinary ability to concentrate and focus their attention, and they can do so for long periods of time, being extremely patient when exploring whatever has captured their interest. This ability allows them to stay with projects long enough to mine gold from them.

HOW THIS ORIENTATION WAKES UP TO THEIR POWER

The journey to empowerment for Type 5s is through sharing their findings with the world. By recognizing the value of their knowledge, and embracing the power of interdependence rather than independence, they can harness their intellectual curiosity to connect with others and make a meaningful impact.

SUPERCONSCIOUS SUPERPOWER / INTUITION STYLE

Knowledge synthesis

Type 5's innate curiosity sends them on a lifelong quest for understanding and competence, and once they become an expert, are able to assimilate their knowledge, grasping complex ideas and distilling them into understandable insights.

Intuitive understanding

They grasp concepts spontaneously and see connections and nuances between seemingly unrelated information.

Expertise

Type 5s are patient teachers who are happy to share their knowledge with those who want to learn.

PATH OF INTEGRATION (FROM DYSFUNCTION TO GENIUS)

DYSFUNCTIONAL

Level 1: Violation

At this stage, Type 5s fear they're incapable of finding a place in the world and may reject all but their most basic needs. They're paranoid and fearful, hoarding their knowledge and harboring extreme distrust of others. They become excessively isolated and plagued by fears.

Level 2: Obsession and compulsion

Their need for knowledge and independence is obsessive and compulsive, leading to a disregard for the well-being of themselves and others. Feeling so small and helpless that almost everything is threatening, they become reclusive, shrinking away from people, consumed by their own increasingly strange thoughts.

Level 3: Pathological destructiveness

In the unhealthiest stage, Type 5s are self-destructive and harmful to others in their pursuit of knowledge and self-sufficiency. Isolated, feeling they can no longer defend themselves from their pain and terror, and wishing to escape from reality, it's possible to suffer psychotic breaks, schizoid withdrawal, or suicide.

FUNCTIONAL

Level 1: Imbalance / social role

In this stage, they fear their skills are insufficient, and they need more preparation before taking their place in the world. Unsure of themselves, they get overly focused on knowledge and independence and might find it challenging to connect with others on an emotional level.

Level 2: Interpersonal control

At this level, Type 5s could struggle to express their emotions and vulnerability, and are overly focused on independence. They fear the needs of others will distract them from their projects to the point it's difficult to form close emotional connections. They minimize their own needs, grow more secretive, and spend more time alone.

Level 3: Overcompensation

There's an obsession with knowledge and independence, fearing others will threaten the niche they've been creating. Their own ideas can be bizarre and disturbing, and they may be scornful of those who can't understand them, so they withdraw from the world. Their isolation can lead to a sense of loneliness and disconnection.

GENIUS

Level 1: Liberation

At their healthiest, Type 5s learn to embrace their inner wisdom and recognize the value of interdependence. Clear-minded and compassionate, they let go of the belief that they're an outside observer and fully engage in life. They're admired for their depth of understanding and capacity to guide others on their quest for knowledge.

Level 2: Psychological capacity

Type 5s develop self-awareness and emotional depth. Smart, curious, and independent, they focus on their environment and feel confident to function in it. They can navigate their own emotions and those of others with authenticity and empathy.

Level 3: Social Value

Type 5s reinforce their self-image by mastering a body of knowledge or skills that makes them competent and strong. They're recognized for their genuine curiosity and capacity to share their knowledge. Exploring original ideas and forms results in groundbreaking inventions and innovative art, inspiring others to new depths of their own minds.

HOW TO HEAL THE WOUND

Healing the wound of a Type 5 involves recognizing their inherent worth and the value of interdependence, understanding that it's acceptable to rely on others and share their knowledge.

Type 5s would benefit from

- realizing that true knowing and understanding come from participation because they can't learn what an experience is like from observation alone;
- understanding that learning through experience is freeing because when you're present, relaxed, and engaged, you develop a deep inner knowing; and
- letting go of the idea that they're separate from their environment and become engaged with reality because they're a part of it.

By getting involved, Type 5s can accept the fullness of the experience without the mental commentary, which is the most freeing and safe experience available.

FAMOUS EXAMPLES OF INVESTIGATORS

Albert Einstein

The iconic physicist, Albert Einstein, epitomizes the Type 5's thirst for knowledge and capacity for groundbreaking discoveries. His revolutionary theories reshaped our understanding of the universe, showcasing the power of intellect and curiosity.

Emily Dickinson

The enigmatic poet, Emily Dickinson, represents the depth and introspection of a Type 5. Her poetry delves into profound themes, reflecting the investigative nature of this personality type.

J. R. R. Tolkien

The celebrated author of books, including *The Hobbit* and *The Lord of the Rings*, is a prime example of the Type 5's capacity for world-building and intricate storytelling. His description of Middle-earth reflects the depth and imagination of this personality type, and his inventive work created languages for the creatures who lived there.

Marie Curie

The pioneering scientist, Marie Curie, exemplifies the Type 5's dedication to knowledge and groundbreaking discoveries. Her work in the field of radioactivity has had a profound and lasting impact on science.

IN SUMMARY

Understanding Enneagram Type 5, the Investigator, offers us a glimpse into a world of relentless curiosity, intellectual depth, and the capacity for profound insights. They excel in their pursuit of knowledge and self-sufficiency but may sometimes grapple with emotional detachment and isolation. By gaining an understanding of hidden and lost messages, and the compensatory strategies they employ, Type 5s can find self-acceptance and a willingness to share their wisdom with the world.

To identify a Type 5, observe their insatiable curiosity, intellectual depth, and preference for solitude.

TEN QUESTIONS TO UNCOVER TYPE 5 TRAITS

1. Are you constantly seeking knowledge and understanding in various aspects of your life?
2. Is your self-worth closely tied to your capacity for self-sufficiency and intellectual depth?
3. Do you often struggle with emotional vulnerability, intimacy, and a desire for solitude?
4. Are you prone to immersing yourself in intellectual pursuits and seeking autonomy in certain areas?
5. Have you ever felt a deep fear of being overwhelmed or incapable of handling life's challenges?
6. Do you frequently believe that you must gather knowledge and be self-sufficient to be valued?
7. Are you often seen as independent and self-reliant, even to the point of appearing detached?

8. Is it challenging for you to rely on others or express your emotions openly?
9. Do you have a strong desire to be knowledgeable, self-sufficient, and independent, even if it means maintaining emotional distance?
10. Have you ever felt a sense of isolation or loneliness, despite your pursuit of knowledge and self-sufficiency?

CHAPTER 10

TYPE 6: THE LOYALIST

"WHAT CAN I BELIEVE IN AND DEFEND?"

Type 6s, the Loyalists, are known for their steadfast commitment to security, a strong sense of loyalty, and a persistent need to anticipate and prepare for potential threats. They're driven by their requirement for safety, cautious approach to life, and staunch allegiance to those they trust. At their best, Type 6s are trustworthy, reliable, and able to demonstrate a steadfast loyalty to the people they love and the causes they believe in.

They often rely on their intuition to anticipate potential dangers and devise contingency plans to mitigate perceived risks. Having an acute sense of what could go wrong, they'll seek to avoid unexpected challenges, should they arise.

At the heart of the Type 6 personality lies a profound belief that they must be prepared for any potential threat or danger, as their survival depends on it. They tend to be vigilant and responsible and often seek guidance and reassurance from trusted authorities.

The other side of the coin is that they're primarily motivated by fear and watchfulness, as they desire safety and predictability in an unpredictable world. They may have difficulty trusting others, and if they feel betrayed, they're likely to react strongly and turn against those they feel have deceived them.

KEY CHARACTERISTICS AND TRAITS

1. Need for security

Type 6s are marked by their deep-seated need to have security and stability in their lives. They often wrestle with concerns about possible threats and what the future might hold.

2. Desire for reassurance

Their core desire is to find reliable sources of guidance and reassurance. They seek trusted individuals, organizations, or systems that can provide them with a sense of safety.

3. Caution and preparedness

They have a tendency to weigh the pros and cons of various scenarios, generally watchful and well-equipped, having anticipated potential dangers and taken steps to mitigate them.

4. Doubt and questioning

Type 6s may engage in extensive questioning and fall into self-doubt, inclined to seek external validation for their decisions and actions.

5. Fear of abandonment

They often grapple with the fear of abandonment and the loss of the support and security they've established, proving a strong sense of loyalty.

6. Loyalty

They might be slow to trust, but once they do, they prefer long-term relationships, whether personal or professional.

7. Commitment to causes

They're frequently dedicated to causes they believe in, becoming dedicated advocates for the protection of others or social justice.

RELATIONSHIP DYNAMICS

In relationships, Type 6s are loyal to those they trust, demonstrating extreme support and commitment.

PERSONALITY PROFILE

- Skeptical
- Slow to trust.
- Risk-avoidant
- Prioritize security
- Analytical
- Phobic
- Timid
- Ingratiating
- Counterphobic
- Abrasive
- Aggressive
- Contrarian

Type 6s lost faith in authority when they were young. They remember being afraid of those who had power over them and being denied agency. Those memories carry over into adult life as mistrust of authority and other people's motives. They aim to ease this sense of insecurity either by behaving dutifully and seeking a strong protector or by being rebellious and defiant.

As a result, there are two kinds of Type 6s–phobic and counterphobic. A phobic Type 6, uncertain of their capacity to act, winds up dithering, replacing action with analysis, and handing over their power to those they see as leaders, while a counterphobic will put their head into the lion's mouth, for example by becoming a skydiving champion to counter a fear of heights.

Both types need to "know the worst." The phobic Type 6 needs this information so they can delay taking action because hazards, whether actual or potential, seem far more real than the promise of success. This means they sometimes need to be put against the wall, so they're forced to act, while the Counterphobic will come up with a plan that sends them headlong into the wall.

HOW TYPE 6S MANIPULATE

Type 6s may manipulate through their doubt and anxiety, seeking reassurance or guidance to alleviate their fears. They can express distrust or skepticism to elicit support or test the reliability of those around them.

BASIC FEAR

Their core fear revolves around the dread of being without the security of someone directing them and not being able to survive on their own.

BASIC DESIRE

Their primary desire is to have guidance and support, to feel secure and taken care of. They yearn for reliable sources of protection and often seek guidance from trusted authorities.

UNCONSCIOUS EGO MESSAGE / MAIN UNCONSCIOUS MESSAGE

Type 6s carry an unconscious message that says, "You're only worthy when you're safe and secure." This message drives their search for security, a need to mitigate risks, and can lead to feelings of inadequacy when they see themselves as being vulnerable.

The childhood experience of feeling unsupported and unguided, and of being unable to survive on your own, isn't limited to Type 6s. However, they hold onto that pattern well into adulthood.

A key factor in letting go of this fear is the presence of a caring authority figure who will provide direction and encouragement, allowing the child to step into the world as an individual, feeling safe in their own guidance and support.

For Type 6s, their own self-comfort is deemed insufficient, so they're always on the hunt for the authority or care they believe they need, which fuels them to keep their guard up and leads to trust anxiety.

Because of their self-doubt, Type 6s believe they lack the internal resources needed to handle life's challenges, so they look for someone or something that will guarantee their safety and security, now and in the future. With their deep fear of abandonment or being left alone, they're relentlessly loyal to no end.

They have a hard time connecting with their inner guidance system and don't have confidence in their own mind and judgment.

LOST CHILDHOOD MESSAGE

You're capable and have the ability to support yourself.

Type 6s were raised in an environment where they needed guidance and security to survive, thus sending them on a lifelong quest for protection and reliability to safeguard their world.

UNPACKING THE UNCONSCIOUS MESSAGE

Let's take a look at what their unconscious message translates to.

Hypervigilance and caution

Type 6s become hyper-vigilant and cautious, always on the lookout for potential risks, and are often well-prepared for a range of possible scenarios.

Doubt and questioning

They tend to question authority, beliefs, and decisions to ensure their safety, which can lead to a sense of skepticism and a reluctance to easily trust.

Seeking security

Type 6s often seek security and assurance in various forms, such as affiliating with dependable individuals and systems or following well-established routines.

Fear of abandonment

The fear of being abandoned or left without support can play a significant role in their lives. They may worry about losing the protection of a trusted source.

ASSUMPTION

Type 6s often assume they must anticipate and prepare for every potential threat to be loved and appreciated. They're the guardians, ever watchful for danger and ready to protect.

COMPENSATING STRATEGY

Type 6s can be either wholly loyal or fiercely confrontational when it comes to authority. They may compensate for their fears by being cautious, faithful, and diligent, or angry and abrasive.

GIFT

Type 6s are endowed with tremendous endurance and achieve their objectives through steady and persistent effort. They pay attention to detail and approach problems carefully and methodically, organizing resources, prioritizing tasks, and believing that their personal value rests on their reliability and the quality of the work they produce.

High-functioning Type 6s respect dependability and good craftsmanship, and, to the best of their ability, provide them. Because of their underlying vigilance and sensitivity to danger signals, they also foresee problems and are natural troubleshooters.

They tend to excel at work that involves careful analysis and an ability to keep track of variables. Their diligence can alert them to discrepancies in systems, potential problems, inaccuracies, or contradictions.

HOW THIS ORIENTATION WAKES UP TO THEIR POWER

Type 6s gain their power by recognizing their own inner strength and ability to provide security. By embracing courage and self-assurance, they can lead with a sense of trust and reliability.

SUPERCONSCIOUS SUPERPOWER / INTUITION STYLE

Threat detection

They have an uncanny ability to sense potential threats and challenges. Their intuition guides them in anticipating danger.

Risk assessment

Their intuition aids them in evaluating situations for potential pitfalls and threats, making them cautious and prepared.

Loyalty intuition

They intuitively recognize people they can trust and rely on their intuition to determine the reliability of those around them.

PATH OF INTEGRATION (FROM DYSFUNCTION TO GENIUS)

DYSFUNCTIONAL

Level 1: Violation

At this stage, Type 6s may become paranoid, fearful, and excessively mistrustful. They intuitively fear their behavior has harmed their own security, so they trust themselves even less. They doubt the intentions of everyone around them and become controlling to protect themselves.

Level 2: Obsession and compulsion

Type 6s become insecure and desperate, believing people will destroy whatever safety they have left. Their fears and anxieties are obsessive and compulsive, leading to a disregard for the well-being of themselves and others. They could become manipulative and seek to control every aspect of their lives, eventually hitting out at enemies, real or imagined.

Level 3: Pathological destructiveness

In the unhealthiest stage, Type 6s can become self-destructive and harmful to others in their quest for security and reassurance. Guilt and self-hatred lead them to punish themselves, inviting disgrace and bringing down all they've achieved. Their paranoia and fear may lead to extreme actions.

FUNCTIONAL

Level 1: Imbalance / social role

In this stage, they fear they'll lose their independence, but also believe they need more support, which makes them overly focused on their doubts and anxieties. Struggling with excessive skepticism, they find it challenging to trust others and are excessively cautious.

Level 2: Interpersonal control

Due to worrying that they can't meet all of their commitments, Type 6s try to resist additional pressures without alienating supporters. They struggle to express their doubts and anxieties openly and have difficulty trusting their own judgment, which makes them constantly seek reassurance. They're anxious, pessimistic, and suspicious, leading to greater caution, impulsiveness, and indecision.

Level 3: Overcompensation

Fearing they're losing the support of their allies, they become unsure of themselves, obsessed with their fears and anxieties, and at times becoming excessively untrusting. Their need for security may lead to a sense of constant anxiety and suspicion. Feeling their good faith has been betrayed, they blame others and get into power struggles.

GENIUS

Level 1: Liberation

At their healthiest, Type 6s let go of the belief that they must rely on someone or something outside of themselves for support and learn to embrace their inner strength and self-assurance. They're secure within themselves, grounded, calm, and brave, and they're admired by others for their wisdom and capacity to guide and protect them.

Level 2: Psychological capacity

They develop self-awareness and emotional depth and can navigate their own emotions, as well as those of others, with authenticity and empathy. They're friendly, trustworthy, and engaging, seeking to build connection and stability in their world.

Level 3: Social Value

Type 6s reinforce their self-image by working to create and sustain mutually beneficial systems. They're disciplined and practical, alert to potential problems, and recognized for their genuine reliability and capacity to create safety. They form alliances, inspiring trust and loyalty in those around them.

HOW TO HEAL THE WOUND

Healing the wound of a Type 6 involves recognizing their inherent worth and the strength they have within, understanding that they're capable of providing their own security and can trust their own judgment.

Type 6s would benefit from

- realizing how supported they actually are at all times, not just by family and friends, but also by the wider world;

- relying on the support of the universe, their body, their inner guidance system, and everything around them;
- understanding that when they try to analyze, strategize, and figure out how to stay safe in the future, while avoiding all pain, they're diminishing the part of the self that knows it will always find a way to be safe; and
- knowing that transformation is achieved when they stop depending on others for security and become their own support and guidance.

Deep down, Type 6s know the universe is benevolent and that they're powerful, intelligent, and able to create the life they desire. They come to understand that real safety, wisdom, and security come from experience.

FAMOUS EXAMPLES OF LOYALISTS

Winston Churchill

The iconic British prime minister Winston Churchill exemplifies the Type 6's capacity for leadership and steadfastness. His allegiance to the safety and security of his country during World War II showcases the Loyalist's dedication to protecting their realm.

Marge Simpson

The beloved character Marge Simpson from *The Simpsons* represents the loyalty and reliability of a Type 6. Her role as the stabilizing force within her family reflects their quintessential characteristics.

Paul Revere

The American patriot Paul Revere embodies the vigilance and dedication of a Type 6. His famous midnight ride during the American Revolution to warn the colonial militia of the approach of British troops reflects the Loyalist's readiness to protect and alert others. The event was commemorated in Henry Wadsworth Longfellow's 1861 poem, "Paul Revere's Ride."

IN SUMMARY

Understanding Enneagram Type 6, the Loyalist, opens the door to a world of unwavering commitment, reliability, and the desire for safety and security. Type 6s excel in their capacity to protect and prepare, but may sometimes grapple with doubt and excessive caution. By gaining an understanding of hidden and lost messages, and the compensatory strategies they employ, Type 6s can achieve self-acceptance and self-assurance.

To identify a Type 6, observe their vigilant nature, loyalty, and tendency to seek guidance and security.

TEN QUESTIONS TO UNCOVER TYPE 6 TRAITS

1. Do you constantly seek security and anticipate potential threats?
2. Is your self-worth closely tied to your capacity to be reliable and vigilant?
3. Do you often struggle with doubt, anxiety, and a need for reassurance?
4. Are you prone to questioning decisions and seeking guidance from trusted authorities or individuals?
5. Have you ever felt a deep fear of being without support or protection?
6. Do you frequently believe that you must anticipate and prepare for potential dangers to be loved and appreciated?
7. Are you often seen as cautious, loyal, and diligent in your responsibilities?
8. Is it challenging for you to trust your own judgment or make decisions without seeking guidance or reassurance?
9. Do you have a strong desire to have direction and support, to feel secure and taken care of?
10. Have you ever felt a sense of constant anxiety or suspicion, despite your vigilant efforts to protect yourself and others?

CHAPTER 11

TYPE 7: THE ENTHUSIAST

"I STILL HAVEN'T FIGURED OUT WHAT I WANT TO BE WHEN I GROW UP."

Type 7s, the Enthusiasts, are characterized by their boundless zest for life, pursuit of adventure, and insatiable hunger for new experiences. They have a lively imagination and a desire to avoid pain and discomfort.

At their best, Type 7s are joyous and adventurous, and capable of inspiring others with their vitality and passion. Joy is their natural state, and they want to make sure everyone feels this way. The counterculture revolution of the 1960s allowed Type 7 ideals to expand in their purest form.

They often rely on their intuition to seek out new opportunities and exciting possibilities, while possessing a keen sense of optimism and a belief in the abundance of the world. They can be naturally inclined toward spontaneity and embrace life.

At the heart of the Type 7 personality is the belief that depending on outside sources for fulfillment isn't acceptable. The other side of the coin is that they're primarily motivated by the desire for freedom and the pursuit of happiness, so they avoid committing to any one thing through fear of missing out and never truly experience anything to full completion.

KEY CHARACTERISTICS AND TRAITS

1. Adventurous spirit

Type 7s are known for their adventurous and open-minded nature. They actively seek out new experiences and opportunities for excitement.

2. Desire for freedom

Their core desire is to maintain a sense of freedom and avoid feeling restricted or confined by obligations, commitments, or negativity.

3. Positive outlook

They possess a naturally positive and optimistic outlook, often reframing challenges as opportunities and focusing on the bright side of situations.

4. Fear of pain and discomfort

Type 7s grapple with a fear of facing pain, discomfort, or negative emotions, which can drive them to escape or avoid difficult situations.

5. Impulsiveness

They could exhibit impulsive behavior, making quick decisions and changes to maintain a sense of excitement and stimulation.

6. Restlessness

Type 7s may experience a constant need for novelty and variety.

7. Commitment issues

They can struggle with commitment, perceiving it as something that limits their freedom and the potential for new experiences.

RELATIONSHIP DYNAMICS

Because they value independence, they're constantly seeking new experiences.

PERSONALITY PROFILE

- Effervescent optimist
- Insatiable appetite for life
- Tries out everything but commits to nothing
- Difficulty remaining in a painful situation long enough to see that a problem exists

Enthusiasts are sustained by the motto that there's no point in a life without adventure. The buoyancy of their belief in life's opportunities is supported by their habit of keeping multiple options open and making backup plans.

Type 7s strive to retain pleasant memories. In childhood, when faced with frightening situations, they calmed their fear by escaping into their imagination. They tended to be lighthearted and sunny, often addicted to planning and play.

They approach life with verve, curiosity, and enthusiasm for anything that captures their attention. Their minds move easily from one idea to another, and they have a hard time staying focused on just one task or project, which means they're fast learners and can quickly become proficient at any task.

Type 7s can harbor a deep sense of anxiety, but instead of dealing with it, they keep their mind busy by starting new projects or going to new places. Their paranoia stays submerged as long as their thinking can be channeled into visionary plans for future success. That said, they don't feel like they know what they really want, so they try everything out and are always searching for stimulation.

Even average Type 7s tend to be creative, but when they're more balanced and rounded, they can be brilliant, multifaceted people. Their varied abilities and interests, enjoyment of work, and extrovert tendencies, often lead to success.

HOW TYPE 7S MANIPULATE

Type 7s can manipulate through their optimism and avoidance of negative emotions. To escape distress, they might downplay or dodge uncomfortable situations and create a facade of constant happiness, or use their enthusiasm to distract themselves and others from deeper issues.

BASIC FEAR

Their core fear revolves around being trapped and in pain or discomfort. They fear being stuck in a mundane routine, unable to experience the wonders of life.

BASIC DESIRE

Their primary desire is to be happy, content, satisfied, and fulfilled. They yearn for a life filled with pleasure and excitement, free from limitations, and often seek new opportunities and experiences.

UNCONSCIOUS EGO MESSAGE / MAIN UNCONSCIOUS MESSAGE

Type 7s carry an unconscious message that declares, "You're only worthy when you're happy and free from pain," which propels their quest for pleasure and can lead to feelings of inadequacy when they experience discomfort or negative emotions.

The pattern established in childhood is based on a largely unconscious feeling of disconnection from a nurturing figure, so they're left with the wound of feeling frustrated with the neglect at what they perceive as too early an age. As a consequence, they decided to nurture themselves. Finding things difficult during the separation phase, they surrounded themselves with toys, games, and playmates to distract themselves from the pain.

As adults, they still seem to be searching for such distractions. However, if they're unable to satisfy that need, they quickly move on to new experiences, ideas, people, or toys to stimulate their minds and allow them to avoid feeling empty.

The core unconscious message for a Type 7 is the belief that they must be independent, and not reliant on anyone or anything else for security and happiness. This message drives their compulsion to avoid commitment to any one person, cause, or path, and to seek out new experiences that keep their spirits buoyed with the belief that you're only good and okay if you feel happy.

LOST CHILDHOOD MESSAGE

Your life can still be fun and happy, even if you sometimes experience pain.

Type 7s were raised in an environment where they were subjected to the idea that to enjoy life, they needed to remain happy at all costs, thus pushing them into a lifelong quest for pleasure and excitement.

UNPACKING THE UNCONSCIOUS MESSAGES

Let's take a look at what their unconscious message translates to.

Seeking pleasure and variety

Type 7s internalize their unconscious message by seeking pleasure, excitement, and a wide array of experiences, fearing that relying on one source for happiness will lead to dissatisfaction.

Avoiding pain and limitation

They often avoid situations that could potentially be painful, limiting, or boring, which can result in a constant pursuit of novelty and fun to escape discomfort.

Optimism and positivity

Type 7s are typically optimistic and maintain a positive outlook. They prefer focusing on the bright side of life and avoiding feelings of negativity.

Fear of missing out

The fear of missing out on opportunities or experiences can also play a significant role in their lives, so they strive to seize every chance for enjoyment.

Assumption

Deep within their psyche, Type 7s often assume that they must seek pleasure and avoid pain to be loved and appreciated, feeling there's a way that they should be, and if they get it wrong, they'll be in trouble.

COMPENSATING STRATEGY

Type 7s may compensate for their fear of discomfort by being cheerful, adventurous, explorers of their own lives, always on the lookout for the next thrill. They develop multiple interests, pull others into believing how great they are at everything, and strive to prove they have it all.

GIFT

Type 7s know that their primary enjoyment of life comes from contributing something to the world. Healthy Sevens would rather design a dress than buy one off the rack or make a movie rather than watch someone else's.

Provided they can prioritize and set limits, Type 7s can excel at multitasking, which allows them to use a variety of skills and see how their different abilities and/or interests are interrelated.

Similarly, they have a talent for generating ideas quickly and spontaneously. They're big-picture people who like getting projects started and are good at brainstorming fresh approaches to problems.

HOW THIS ORIENTATION WAKES UP TO THEIR POWER

Type 7s gain their power by embracing their emotional depth and learning to sit with discomfort. In this way, they can find contentment and joy in the simplicity of existence.

SUPERCONSCIOUS SUPERPOWER / INTUITION STYLE

Type 7s possess an intuitive sense for exploring the endless possibilities life has to offer. They're visionaries and often see potential opportunities where others might not. Their intuition drives them toward adventure, excitement, and the pursuit of enjoyment.

Opportunity identification

Type 7s are intuitive when it comes to spotting opportunities and possibilities. They can identify potential adventures, activities, and exciting prospects.

Creative vision

Their intuition guides them in creative endeavors, intuitively seeing how to turn their visions into reality.

Adaptability

Type 7s possess an intuitive knack for adapting to new situations, quickly navigating change, and embracing diverse experiences.

PATH OF INTEGRATION (FROM DYSFUNCTION TO GENIUS)

DYSFUNCTIONAL

Level 1: Violation

In this stage, Type 7s may become reckless and impulsive, constantly seeking stimulation. They can fear their actions are bringing them pain and unhappiness, which is possible, as paradoxically, they avoid discomfort to the point of damaging themselves and everyone around them. They're highly impulsive and irresponsible and do whatever promises temporary relief from their anxiety, but this brings them no happiness.

Level 2: Obsession and compulsion

Type 7s can be so desperate to escape their anxiety, they fly out of control, recklessly acting out their pain rather than feeling it. Their pursuit of pleasure and avoidance of discomfort becomes obsessive and compulsive, leading to a disregard for their own well-being and that of others. They may become addicted to constant stimulation, increasingly unstable and erratic, harming themselves or others in the process.

Level 3: Pathological destructiveness

In the unhealthiest stage, Type 7s can be self-destructive and harmful to others in their relentless quest to experience pleasure and avoid pain and discomfort. Their excesses may result in severe financial and physical problems and even chronic pain. They're panic-stricken, believing they're out of options, and feel trapped.

FUNCTIONAL

Level 1: Imbalance / social role

In this stage, Type 7s may fear they're missing out on other, more worthwhile experiences, and become overly focused on seeking pleasure and avoiding discomfort. The struggle with impulsivity keeps them busy, so they could find it challenging to confront deeper emotional issues.

Level 2: Interpersonal control

Type 7s worry they'll become bored or frustrated, and painful feelings will arise, so they try to keep themselves excited and occupied. They may struggle to express negative emotions and constantly seek external stimulation while finding it difficult to confront their own discomfort and use distractions to avoid facing their feelings.

Level 3: Overcompensation

They become excessively impulsive, and their avoidance of pain can lead to a sense of emptiness and an inability to find genuine happiness. They can also be demanding but are seldom satisfied when their demands are met.

GENIUS

Level 1: Liberation

At their healthiest, Type 7s relinquish the belief that they require specific objects and experiences to feel fulfilled, and learn to embrace the joy of life in the present moment, appreciating every experience for what it is. They become grateful, carefree, and admired for their enthusiasm and capacity to help others find enjoyment in the simplest moments.

Level 2: Psychological capacity

They cultivate self-awareness and emotional depth, navigating their own emotions and those of others with authenticity and empathy. Excited by the world of possibilities, they're happy, spontaneous, and outgoing.

Level 3: Social value

Type 7s are recognized for their genuine optimism and capacity to inspire happiness and enthusiasm in those around them. They reinforce their self-image by fully engaging in life with passionate gusto and doing activities that fulfill their needs. They're a source of inspiration and a reminder of the beauty of existence

HOW TO HEAL THE WOUND

Healing the wound of a Type 7 involves recognizing their inherent worth and the beauty of life, even in moments of discomfort. Once they understand that it's acceptable to experience pain and that genuine happiness can be found in the simplicity of existence, they'll embrace the idea that the thrill isn't in the constant pursuit of pleasure but in the richness of every moment.

Type 7s would benefit from

- accepting that the pain they've experienced has already happened, was survivable, and no longer needs to be avoided;
- being present with the pain long enough to realize that it loses its power;
- learning that grieving involves presence and allowing it to heal takes time;
- knowing that directly chasing happiness and satisfaction will never achieve healing because reaching a sense of fulfillment means allowing the richness of the present moment to touch them; and
- understanding that there's nothing wrong with thinking about the future, but it's the primary way you lose your connection with the present.

FAMOUS EXAMPLES OF ENTHUSIASTS

Richard Branson

Entrepreneur and adventurer Richard Branson epitomizes the Type 7's pursuit of pleasure and excitement. His endeavors in business and space travel showcase the boundless enthusiasm and zest for life that this personality type embodies.

Jim Carrey

The iconic comedian and actor Jim Carrey represents the joyful and spontaneous nature of a Type 7. His ability to bring laughter and excitement to his performances reflects the quintessential Enthusiast's characteristics.

Walt Disney

The visionary creator Walt Disney's imaginative and optimistic nature captures the essence of a Type 7. His creation of the Disney theme parks and the magic of animation reflects an Enthusiast's capacity for bringing enjoyment and adventure to life.

Pharrell Williams

The talented musician and producer Pharrell Williams, with his creativity, optimism, and zest for life, is a great depiction of a Type 7. His music and work in the entertainment industry exude the enthusiasm this personality type embodies.

IN SUMMARY

Understanding Enneagram Type 7, the Enthusiast, opens the door to a world of boundless joy, optimism, and the desire for new experiences. They excel in their capacity to find happiness in every area of life, but may sometimes battle restlessness and a constant aversion to discomfort. By gaining an understanding of hidden and lost messages, and the compensatory strategies they employ, Type 7s can remain on the path of self-acceptance and contentment.

To identify a Type Seven, look for their boundless enthusiasm, zest for life, and spontaneous approach to new opportunities.

TEN QUESTIONS TO UNCOVER TYPE 7 TRAITS

1. Are you constantly seeking pleasure and new experiences in various aspects of your life?
2. Is your self-worth closely tied to your capacity to be joyful and avoid discomfort?
3. Do you often struggle with restlessness, a fear of missing out, and an aversion to negative emotions?
4. Are you prone to spontaneity and a desire for constant excitement and adventure?
5. Have you ever felt a deep fear of being trapped in a routine or missing out on life's pleasures?

6. Do you frequently believe that you must constantly seek happiness and avoid discomfort to be loved and appreciated?
7. Are you often seen as optimistic, enthusiastic, and spontaneous in your approach to life?
8. Is it challenging for you to confront discomfort or negative emotions, often seeking external stimulation or distractions to avoid them?
9. Do you have a strong desire to be joyful, content, and free from limitations, seeking new opportunities and experiences?
10. Have you ever felt a sense of emptiness or a constant need for stimulation, despite your pursuit of pleasure and excitement?

CHAPTER 12

TYPE 8: THE PROTECTOR

"I'M THE CONTROLLER OF MY FATE."

Type 8s, the Protectors, are characterized by their unwavering strength, assertiveness, and indomitable spirit. They're known for their toughness, confidence, and need to protect and control their environment.

At their best, Type 8s are powerful, courageous, and capable of inspiring and protecting others. They're deeply concerned with ensuring those they care about aren't hurt or taken advantage of, don't want to be controlled in any way, and won't allow others to have power over them.

They often rely on their intuition to assess situations, recognize potential threats, and make quick decisions, possessing a keen sense of power dynamics and seeking to maintain control in their interactions.

At the core of the Type 8 personality lies a profound belief that vulnerability and trust aren't safe. They only feel secure when they can control a situation by calling the shots and making other people obey.

The other side of the coin is that they're primarily motivated by the desire for control and autonomy. Much of their behavior is involved in making sure they retain and increase whatever power they have for as long as possible. Being in charge is important to them because they're natural leaders and tend to be strong-willed, decisive, and protective of those they care about.

KEY CHARACTERISTICS AND TRAITS

1. Assertiveness

Type 8s are renowned for their assertive and direct nature. They're not afraid to speak their minds, take charge, and confront challenges head-on.

2. Desire for control

Their core desire is to maintain control over their lives and protect themselves and their loved ones from harm or vulnerability.

3. Independence

They value their independence and often resist any form of oppression or control from others.

4. Fear of weakness

Type 8s grapple with a fear of appearing weak or vulnerable, which can lead to a tendency to suppress their own vulnerability and emotions.

5. Protectiveness

They often exhibit a strong protective instinct toward those they care about, aiming to ensure their safety and well-being.

6. Challenge-seeking

They have a penchant for taking on challenges and pushing boundaries in pursuit of their goals.

7. Direct communication

Type 8s are known for their straightforward and direct communication style, which can sometimes lead to conflict, due to their frankness.

RELATIONSHIP DYNAMICS

In relationships, love is more often expressed through protection than demonstrations of tender feelings, meaning they can close themselves off so as not to appear vulnerable.

PERSONALITY PROFILE

- Confrontational
- Overtly angry
- Combative
- Pushy.
- Powerful
- Dominating
- Self-confident
- Decisive
- Willful

Type 8s often describe a combative childhood, where the strong were respected, and the weak were not. Expecting to be disadvantaged, they learned to protect themselves, becoming highly sensitized to the negative intentions of others.

The Type 8 child struggled against a sense of unfair odds and survived by adopting any form of confrontation that would make enemies back down. Their world felt dominated by bigger, stronger people who wanted to control their lives. These are children who've learned to deny their personal limitations to appear strong and lived in denial of personal limitations, which led to a parallel habit of denying their own physical and emotional pain.

Their preferred state of existence is highly amped, fully energized forward motion. Once a desire takes hold, they take action quickly before frustration sets in. They have enormous willpower and vitality, enjoy taking on big projects, and challenge others to do the same.

HOW TYPE 8S MANIPULATE

Type 8s may manipulate through their assertiveness and control, seeking to maintain dominance and power in their relationships by using their strength and directness to influence others or assert their authority.

BASIC FEAR

Their core fear revolves around the dread of being harmed, manipulated, or controlled by others, and appearing weak or vulnerable.

BASIC DESIRE

Their primary desire is to be strong and in control, determine their own course in life, and protect themselves and those they care about. They yearn for a life marked by autonomy and justice, often seeking to empower and defend those in need.

UNCONSCIOUS EGO MESSAGE / MAIN UNCONSCIOUS MESSAGE

Type 8s carry an unconscious message that says, "You're only worthy when you're strong and in control." This message propels their need for authority and can lead to feelings of inadequacy when they experience vulnerability.

In childhood, they felt they had to become adults at an early age. They may have had to deal with a dangerous, erratic, or violent life, and some met the need by not appearing vulnerable or showing weakness.

Their main focus is survival through being powerful. They believe that it's not safe to be gentle, soft, or weak, and it's best not to let down their guard or give the power to hurt them to anyone else. At some point, they felt betrayed and decided they would never be betrayed again. They accepted this was the way life was going to be and became hard and remorseless towards others who appeared vulnerable or weak.

The core unconscious message for a Type 8 is the belief that they're not worthy of love if they're vulnerable and not in control. This message propels their need for leadership and to protect others while appearing independent and invulnerable because you're only good and okay if you're strong and in control of your situation.

LOST CHILDHOOD MESSAGE

You're protected and loved, no matter what.

Type 8s were raised in an environment where they needed to be strong to protect themselves, thus pushing them into a lifelong quest for authority and control.

UNPACKING THE UNCONSCIOUS MESSAGE

Let's take a look at what their unconscious message translates to.

Strength and independence

Type 8s internalize this message by striving to be strong, self-reliant, and independent, fearing that vulnerability and trust may lead to betrayal or harm.

Assertiveness and control

They often adopt an assertive, take-charge approach to maintain control over their environment and protect themselves while avoiding any sense of powerlessness.

Protection and loyalty

Type 8s are fiercely protective of their loved ones and value loyalty and trustworthiness in those they choose as confidants.

Avoiding weakness

The fear of appearing weak or helpless drives them to suppress vulnerability and maintain a strong facade.

ASSUMPTION

Deep within their psyche, Type 8s often assume they must assert themselves and maintain power to be loved and appreciated. Only the dominant get what they want, so if they don't dominate, they'll be subjugated, which means they're always on guard and ready to defend their people and territory.

COMPENSATING STRATEGY

Type 8s often compensate for their fear of vulnerability by being assertive, protective, and direct. They constantly align with those in power and in control, to regulate their environment and protect themselves and those they care about.

GIFT

Type 8s are people of action and practical intuition. They have vision and derive great satisfaction from being constructive. both literally and figuratively. A key element of their leadership is their practical creativity. They enjoy building things from the ground up and are able to see possibilities in people and situations.

They like to offer incentives and challenges that bring out people's abilities and positive qualities. In this way, they help others to recognize resources and strengths they didn't know they possessed. Therefore, the key word for Type 8s is *empowerment*.

Control, in a healthy Type 8, takes the form of self-mastery. They're magnanimous and big-hearted, possessing a generosity that allows them to transcend their self-interest. On a deeper level, the ultimate goal is the desire to have a beneficial influence on people and their world.

HOW THIS ORIENTATION WAKES UP TO THEIR POWER

The journey to empowerment for Type 8s is by embracing their own vulnerability and recognizing the value of compassion and cooperation. In this way, they can lead with a sense of fairness and justice, acknowledging that true strength is found in unity and shared responsibility.

SUPERCONSCIOUS SUPERPOWER / INTUITION STYLE

Power dynamics

Type 8s are highly intuitive in their understanding of power dynamics. They can assess authority and control in a range of diverse situations.

Influence

Their intuition guides them in understanding how to influence others and assert their authority effectively.

Protection instinct

Type 8s possess an instinctive drive to protect and empower those they care about. They can sense when their loved ones need support and act on it.

PATH OF INTEGRATION (FROM DYSFUNCTION TO GENIUS)

DYSFUNCTIONAL

Level 1: Violation

In this stage, fearing others are turning against them, Type 8s may be aggressive, domineering, and excessively focused on maintaining power and control. They could feel betrayed and unable to trust anyone, so they become determined to protect themselves at any cost, causing them to disregard the well-being of others and harm themselves in the process.

Level 2: Obsession and compulsion

Type 8s can become so desperate to protect themselves and fearful of retaliation, that they attack potential rivals before they can be threatened by them. Their pursuit of control and dominance may become obsessive and compulsive to the point they're addicted to their own authority, to the detriment of themselves and those around them.

Level 3: Pathological destructiveness

In their unhealthiest stage, Type 8s can become self-destructive and harmful to others in their relentless quest for control and dominance. They try to destroy everything rather than let anyone triumph over or control them. Their aggression and disregard for vulnerability, remorselessly trampling everything in their path, may lead to extreme actions.

FUNCTIONAL

Level 1: Imbalance / social role

In this stage, Type 8s could begin to fear they don't have sufficient resources to succeed with their projects or carry out their role as providers. They may become overly focused on control and dominance, sometimes struggling with confrontational behavior and finding it challenging to be open to vulnerability, so they suppress their own emotions.

Level 2: Interpersonal control

Type 8s may worry that people won't respect them or give them their due, so they try to convince everyone of their importance. They boast, bluff, and make big promises to get people aligned with their plans, wanting them to know they're in charge.

Level 3: Overcompensation

Type 8s may become afraid that others aren't backing them up, so they apply pressure to make people do what they want, at times being excessively confrontational, controlling, and dominant. Their fear of vulnerability may lead to a sense of isolation and an inability to find true connection.

GENIUS

Level 1: Liberation

At their healthiest, Type 8s learn to let go of the belief that they must always be in control of their environment, embrace vulnerability, and recognize the strength in cooperation and compassion. They're magnanimous, courageous, and forgiving, admired for their fairness and capacity to protect and empower others.

Level 2: Psychological capacity

They cultivate self-awareness and emotional depth by using their energy and willpower to become independent and gain authority over their lives. They're assertive, direct, and resourceful, and can navigate their own emotions, as well as those of others, with authenticity and empathy.

Level 3: Social value

When they're at their healthiest, Type 8s reinforce their self-image by taking on challenges and are recognized for their genuine assertiveness, as well as their capacity to bring justice and protection to those in need. They bring out people's strengths, becoming a source of inspiration and a reminder of the power found in unity and shared responsibility.

HOW TO HEAL THE WOUND

Healing the wound of a Type 8 involves recognizing that vulnerability isn't a weakness but a source of strength and connection. They need to understand that true power lies in the ability to be open and to share their burdens with others, not through forcefulness or trying to bend situations to their will, and that controlling situations or people is actually a form of imprisonment.

Type 8s would benefit from

- understanding that being vulnerable is the strongest position because always needing to be strong makes people hard and brittle, so they break
- recognizing that the strongest leader has the courage to be vulnerable and can play whatever role is needed
- letting their vulnerability come through and that by stepping into the hurt, they're able to be liber-

ated from the fear of being weak and powerless, and thus regain their true power.

In their deeper self, Type 8s can remember the simple joy of existence, of being alive, and they have some level of connection with that primal sense of the innocence of being a child, which means it's now safe for them to explore again. They come to discover that by allowing themselves to give in to this side of themselves, they're more courageous and stronger than someone who's unable to.

FAMOUS EXAMPLES OF PROTECTORS

Frank Sinatra

The legendary singer and entertainer Frank Sinatra embodies the assertiveness and authority of a Type 8. His iconic presence in the music industry and his determination to control his career reflect the essence of a Protector.

Queen Latifah

The versatile artist Queen Latifah represents the strength, leadership, and courage of a Type 8. Her achievements in music and acting and her advocacy for social justice highlight the assertiveness and directness that Protectors often possess.

Eleanor Roosevelt

The former American First Lady Eleanor Roosevelt exemplifies the protective and justice-seeking nature of a Type 8. Her advocacy for human rights, strong leadership in politics, and commitment to defending those in need are typical of a Protector.

IN SUMMARY

Understanding Enneagram Type 8, the Protector, opens the door to a world of unwavering strength, assertiveness, and the pursuit of justice. They excel in their capacity to protect and empower, but may sometimes grapple with vulnerability and an excessive need for control. By gaining an understanding of hidden and lost messages, and the compensatory strategies they employ, Type 8s can embark on a journey of self-acceptance and vulnerability.

To identify a Type 8, observe their strength, assertiveness, and directness in pursuing justice.

TEN QUESTIONS TO UNCOVER TYPE 8 TRAITS

1. Are you constantly seeking control and assertiveness in various aspects of your life?
2. Is your self-worth closely tied to your capacity to be strong and in control?

3. Do you often struggle with vulnerability, a fear of weakness, and a tendency to guard your emotions?
4. Are you prone to assertiveness and a desire for autonomy and justice?
5. Have you ever felt a deep fear of being controlled, manipulated, or vulnerable?
6. Do you frequently believe that you must assert yourself and maintain control to be loved and appreciated?
7. Are you often seen as strong, assertive, and direct in your approach to life?
8. Is it challenging for you to be open and vulnerable or share your burdens with others, often seeking to maintain dominance and power in your relationships?
9. Do you have a strong desire to be autonomous and strong and protect yourself and those you care about, often seeking to empower and defend those in need?
10. Have you ever felt a sense of isolation or a constant desire for control and dominance, despite your pursuit of autonomy and justice?

CHAPTER 13

TYPE 9: THE PEACEMAKER

"WE CAN ALL GET ALONG."

Type 9s, the Peacemakers, are characterized by their deep desire for harmony, ability to mediate, and an innate capacity for finding common ground. They possess a love of peace and a tendency to avoid conflict.

At their best, Type 9s are cordial, accepting, and capable of bringing people together in a spirit of unity and cooperation. They tend to be easygoing and accommodating and strive to maintain a sense of serenity in their lives.

They often rely on their intuition to assess situations, recognize potential conflict, and find ways to create accord. Possessing a keen sense of balance, they'll often seek to mediate and accommodate differing viewpoints.

At the core of the Type 9 personality lies a profound belief that their presence is inconsequential, and maintaining peace is of the utmost importance. The other side of the coin is that they're primarily motivated by the desire for inner and outer peace while trying to ignore the disturbing aspects of life by living in a state of passivity or gross denial. Saying "no" to someone can feel as disappointing as being denied something for themselves.

KEY CHARACTERISTICS AND TRAITS

1. Love of harmony

Type 9s are known for their love of harmony and their natural ability to mediate and bring people together.

2. Desire for peace

Their core desire is to maintain a sense of inner and outer peace, avoiding conflict and discord whenever possible.

3. Easygoing nature

They often possess an easygoing and adaptable disposition, making them pleasant to be around.

4. Avoidance of conflict

Type 9s tend to avoid conflict and confrontation, sometimes at the expense of expressing their true feelings and needs.

5. Tendency to merge

They have a tendency to merge with the desires and opinions of others, at times losing their own sense of self in the process.

6. Procrastination

Type 9s may procrastinate or delay taking action when faced with tasks or decisions that could disrupt their serenity.

7. Conflict avoidance

They struggle with potential conflict, avoiding difficult conversations and suppressing their own needs to maintain harmony.

RELATIONSHIP DYNAMICS

In relationships, Type 9s can be easygoing and cordial, but may submerge their true feelings for the sake of maintaining the peace.

PERSONALITY PROFILE

- Passive-aggressive
- Decidedly unambitious
- Shy and retiring
- Withdrawn
- Attracted to peaceful environments and endeavors
- Dreamers
- Easygoing
- Receptive
- Reassuring,
- Agreeable
- Complacent

Type 9s are the children who felt overlooked when they were young, remembering that their point of view was seldom sought or heard and that other people's needs were deemed more important than their own.

Eventually, they became preoccupied with small comforts and substitutes for love. Realizing that their own priorities were likely to be discounted, they learned to numb themselves, divert their energy from priorities, and forget themselves.

They tend to go along with everyone else's agendas. Believing that their own position will be discounted, but still wanting to maintain connection, they've learned to incorporate other people's enthusiasms as their own.

They take refuge in the safety of not knowing what they want, not having a position to defend, and staying in an uncommitted limbo where decisions are still pending. Once a position has been established, they can be just as stubborn about holding onto it as they were against having to choose it. Their most natural state of mind is on the fence.

Type 9s are called Peacemakers precisely because their natural ambivalence allows them to both agree and yet not fully commit to any one point of view.

HOW TYPE 9S MANIPULATE

Type 9s can manipulate through their agreeableness and accommodation, often suppressing their own desires to maintain peace. They might avoid conflict by going along with the wishes of others or sidestepping difficult conversations, and could also use their adaptability to maintain a facade of agreement and tranquility.

BASIC FEAR

Their core fear revolves around the dread of conflict, disharmony, or disruption of their inner peace. They worry about loss and separation.

BASIC DESIRE

Their primary desire is to maintain peace, harmony, and a sense of unity. They yearn for a life marked by peace of mind, tranquility, and cooperation, often seeking to mediate and accommodate conflicting parties.

UNCONSCIOUS EGO MESSAGE / MAIN UNCONSCIOUS MESSAGE

Type 9s carry an unconscious message that says, "You're only worthy when you keep the peace and avoid conflict," which drives their need for harmony and can lead to feelings of inadequacy when experiencing discord.

Their childhood coping pattern involved disassociating from the threatening and traumatic events around them and becoming the peacemaker or mediator during family conflict. They learned the easiest way to keep harmony in the family was to disappear and not cause trouble.

By remaining undemanding and low maintenance, with few expectations, they could effectively protect themselves and keep the peace. They grew up with the feeling that asserting themselves created difficulties and was not allowed, so they stayed in the background, eventually becoming unable to hear the voice of their own wants, needs, and desires. This led to them repressing their anger and adjusting to whatever life presented to them, constantly telling themselves, "You're okay if those around you are okay."

LOST CHILDHOOD MESSAGE

Your needs matter.

Type 9s were raised in an environment where they felt they had to keep the peace to avoid conflicts, thus propelling them into a lifelong quest for harmony and consensus.

UNPACKING THE UNCONSCIOUS MESSAGE

Let's take a look at what their unconscious message translates to.

Avoidance and denial

Type 9s avoid conflict and minimize their own desires and needs, fearing that by asserting themselves, they will disrupt the peace.

Accommodation and harmony

They often prioritize accommodating others and maintaining harmony in their relationships, often going to great lengths to prevent disagreements.

Lack of self-assertion

Type 9s may struggle with asserting themselves and expressing their own desires. They could have difficulty identifying their own needs and wants.

Indecision and inertia

The fear of conflict and wanting to keep the peace can lead to indecision and inertia, which makes it challenging to take action.

ASSUMPTION

Deep within their psyche, Type 9s often assume they must mediate and accommodate to be loved and appreciated. They feel that if conflict or tension is present, they won't get what they want, and since expressing what they want creates conflict or tension, the only way to get it is to not let on that they want it.

COMPENSATING STRATEGY

Type 9s often compensate for their fear of conflict by being agreeable, adaptable, and accommodating. In seeking to create a sense of calm and unity, they don't take many actions, which leads to filling up their time with inessential activities.

GIFT

Type 9s bring people together and resolve conflict by seeing all sides of a situation. They have the ability to relax and take life as it comes.

A great source of strength for their profound patience is a deep "letting be" of other people that allows them to develop in their own way, supported by quiet strength and tremendous endurance. They're able to "hang tough" through hardships and difficulties.

Healthy Type 9s work steadily and persistently toward their goals and often achieve them. Their willpower is liberated, and they discover incredible grit and stamina. They're also effective in handling crises because they have extraordinary inner stability. When others are overreacting with anxiety, Type 9s become the still, calm center that moves ahead and gets things done.

HOW THIS ORIENTATION WAKES UP TO THEIR POWER

The journey to empowerment for a Type 9 is through embracing the existence and importance of their own desires and needs, which allows them to lead with a sense of self-assuredness and assertiveness, while still fostering harmony.

SUPERCONSCIOUS SUPERPOWER / INTUITION STYLE

Conflict detection

Type 9s have an intuitive sense for detecting underlying conflicts and tensions. They can sense when disharmony is present.

Mediation

Their intuition guides them in mediating conflicts and bringing accord to a situation by using their intuitive understanding of how to restore tranquility.

Peaceful cooperation

They possess an intuitive knack for facilitating peaceful cooperation, sensing when collaboration is needed, and helping to bring people together.

PATH OF INTEGRATION (FROM DYSFUNCTION TO GENIUS)

DYSFUNCTIONAL

Level 1: Violation

In this stage, Type 9s may fear that reality will force them to deal with their problems, so they become disengaged, depressed, and excessively focused on avoiding conflict. They disregard their own desires and needs, defending the illusion that everything is okay and stubbornly resisting all efforts to get them to confront their problems, which can lead to them harming themselves or those around them in their quest for peace.

Level 2: Obsession and compulsion

Their pursuit of harmony and accommodation becomes obsessive and compulsive, leading to a disregard for their own well-being and the well-being of others. They can become addicted to passivity and may do damage to themselves or others in the process.

Level 3: Pathological destructiveness

In the unhealthiest stage, Type 9s can become self-destructive and harmful to those around them in their relentless goal to avoid conflict. They try to block out awareness of anything that could affect them through dissociation and denial, often experiencing amnesia, while the passivity and suppression of their own desires could lead to extreme actions.

FUNCTIONAL

Level 1: Imbalance / social role

In this stage, Type 9s may begin to fear conflicts in their lives will ruin their peace of mind, so they become overly focused on accommodating others. They find it challenging to assert their own desires, struggling with passivity and suppressing their own needs. And because they consider many matters not worth arguing about, they'll say yes to things they don't want to do.

Level 2: Interpersonal control

Type 9s may worry that if they make significant changes in their world or express strong feelings, it will disrupt their peace. In an effort to avoid asserting themselves, they seek to maintain harmony by going along with the wishes of others and lose themselves in comforting routines and habits, tuning out problems.

Level 3: Overcompensation

They become obsessed with being accommodating, afraid others will demand responses that will arouse anxiety and ruin their inner serenity. Their fear of conflict and having a strong need to suppress their own desires could lead them to downplay the importance of some problems while trying to deflect others. Unable to assert themselves, they get excessively passive and rely on stoicism to get through all interactions.

GENIUS

Level 1: Liberation

At their healthiest, Type 9s let go of the belief that their participation in the world is unimportant or unwanted, and learn to embrace expressing their wants and needs, while fostering goodwill. They're confident, calm, and present, admired for their self-assuredness and capacity to create unity and tranquility.

Level 2: Psychological capacity

At this level, they focus holistically on the environment or relationships, cultivating self-awareness and emotional depth. They can navigate their own emotions and those of others with authenticity and empathy. Stable, easygoing, and kind, they seek to maintain harmonious stability within themselves and in their environment.

Level 3: Social value

Type 9s learn to reinforce their self-image by creating and maintaining peace and harmony in their world. They use their patient, level-headed approach to mediate conflicts and soothe others, and are recognized for their genuine empathy and capacity to bring people together, becoming a source of inspiration and a reminder of the strength found in cooperation and unity.

HOW TO HEAL THE WOUND

Healing the wound of a Type 9 involves recognizing that the presence of conflict and the assertion of their own desires aren't inherently negative conditions. They need to understand that true peace can only be achieved when they honor their own needs and speak their truth.

Type 9s would benefit from

- letting go of the belief that their participation in the world is unimportant
- believing that achieving unity fulfills everyone's true desires and potential, including their own
- understanding that if everyone just checked out, there would be nothing left

- achieving true connection and wholeness by embracing the human condition fully, connecting with their self, dreams, desires, and even their pain.

Type 9s don't need to forget their needs and desires to create peace. They need to remember the fullness of who and what they truly are.

FAMOUS EXAMPLES OF PEACEMAKERS

Dalai Lama

The spiritual leader Dalai Lama represents the peace, harmony, and desire for unity that a Type 9 often embodies. His commitment to nonviolence and reconciliation and his ability to mediate conflicts reflect the tranquil nature of a Peacemaker.

Mister Rogers

The beloved television host Fred Rogers exemplifies the patience, empathy, and ability to create an understanding that a Peacemaker often possesses. His commitment to fostering sympathy and compassion are the distinctive characteristics of this type.

Audrey Hepburn

The iconic actress Audrey Hepburn showcased the adaptability, grace, and capacity to bring people together that a

Type 9 often exhibits. Her work as a UNICEF Goodwill Ambassador and her dedication to humanitarian causes reflect her peacemaking qualities.

Eckhart Tolle

The spiritual teacher and author Eckhart Tolle embodies the serenity, self-awareness, and capacity to find inner peace that reflect the wonderful qualities the Peacemaker possesses. His work in promoting mindfulness and his ability to bring tranquility to his audience resonates with Type 9's harmonious qualities.

IN SUMMARY

Understanding Enneagram Type 9, the Peacemaker, opens the door to a world of tranquility, empathy, and the pursuit of harmony. They excel in their capacity to create unity, but may sometimes grapple with complacency and a tendency to avoid conflict. By gaining an understanding of hidden and lost messages, and the compensatory strategies they employ, Type 9s can embark on a journey of self-acceptance and self-assertion.

To identify a Type 9, observe their adaptability, empathy, and ability to mediate conflicts.

TEN QUESTIONS TO UNCOVER TYPE 9 TRAITS

1. Are you constantly seeking harmony and the avoidance of conflict in various aspects of your life?
2. Is your self-worth closely tied to your capacity to keep the peace and create unity?
3. Do you often struggle with complacency, a fear of conflict, and a tendency to lose your own identity in the process?
4. Are you prone to adaptability and a desire for tranquility and cooperation?
5. Have you ever felt a deep fear of conflict, disharmony, or disruption of your inner peace?
6. Do you frequently believe that you must mediate and accommodate to be loved and appreciated?
7. Are you often seen as patient, empathetic, and a skilled mediator in your approach to life?
8. Is it challenging for you to assert your own desires or speak your own truth, so you often seek to maintain peace and avoid conflicts in your relationships?
9. Do you have a strong desire to maintain peace, harmony, and a sense of unity, often attempting to mediate and accommodate differing viewpoints?
10. Have you ever felt a sense of inner numbness or a constant need for harmony and accommodation, despite your pursuit of tranquility and cooperation?

CHAPTER 14

THE SUPERCONSCIOUS RESET EXERCISE

Now that you have an understanding of the nine orientations, how you're living in your shadow, the wound, and the superconscious superpower, it's time to reset.

You may feel confident that you've identified your main Enneagram type, or you could be vacillating between two or more potentials. For this exercise, it actually doesn't matter whether you know or not. The first step in creating anything, no matter how big or small you deem your desired end result to be, is to neutralize your shadow. Shedding light on it will make it disappear. You'll learn to assimilate it, and the wound will become your superpower.

Before I get into the main exercise, I want to pre-frame it, so you fully understand what's going on and feel comfortable enough to get the most out of the process.

EXERCISE PREFRAME

Let me quickly recap the Enneagram types.

TYPE 1: THE PERFECTIONIST

Unconscious message: "I'm not perfect."

Unconscious wound: "I'm inherently flawed."

Core belief: "I must be good and get it right."

Superpower: moral compass, injustice detector, and standards of excellence.

TYPE 2: THE HELPER

Unconscious message: "I'm not worthy."

Unconscious wound: "I'm unlovable and have to be needed."

Core belief: "I must meet the needs of others to earn love."

Superpower: empathy, emotional insights, relationship harmonizer.

TYPE 3: THE ACHIEVER

Unconscious message: "I must achieve."

Unconscious wound: "I'm worthless and unimportant unless I'm successful and admirable to others."

Core belief: "I need to achieve to be worthy of love and respect."

Superpowers: intuitive grasp of success, self-presentation, success mapping, and understanding of market trends.

TYPE 4: THE ROMANTIC

Unconscious message: "I'm different."

Unconscious wound: "I don't belong."

Core belief: "I must continue to express my individuality and creativity in the world."

Superpowers: authenticity radar, creative expression, emotional depth.

TYPE 5: THE INVESTIGATOR

Unconscious message: "I'm not capable."

Unconscious wound: "I lack inner resources."

Core belief: "I must possess knowledge."

Superpower: knowledge synthesis, intuitive understanding, and being an expert in multiple subjects.

TYPE 6: THE LOYALIST

Unconscious message: "I'm not safe."

Unconscious wound: "Without guidance or support, I'm vulnerable to danger."

Core belief: "I must seek security and guidance from an authority figure."

Superpower: threat detection, risk assessment, and loyalty intuition.

TYPE 7: THE ENTHUSIAST

Unconscious message: "I'm not allowed to be sad."

Unconscious wound: "I'm deprived or in pain, and I need to escape it."

Core belief: "I must seek pleasure."

Superpower: intuitive exploration of possibilities, adaptability, creative vision, and opportunity identification.

TYPE 8: THE PROTECTOR

Unconscious Message: "I am powerless."

Unconscious wound: "I'm vulnerable and weak."

Core belief: "I must be in control and powerful."

Superpower: intuitive mastery of control, power dynamics, influence, and protection instinct.

TYPE 9: THE PEACEMAKER

Unconscious message: "I'm nobody."

Unconscious wound: "I'm disconnected or in conflict with others."

Core belief: "I must maintain inner and outer peace."

Superpower: conflict detection, mediation, and harmonizer.

HOW CAN I ACCEPT THE TRUTH?

The answer is that you must die to the wound and not try to fix it. You see, by trying to change it, you're just a kid running away from the reality of it. The wound isn't right or wrong, good or bad. It just is.

When you let go of thinking that you can't handle the truth of your wound, then you're free from it. The more you try to be successful in an attempt to push the wound away, the more it will be there. The more effort you put into becoming perfect and escaping it, the more you're teaching yourself that you're imperfect, which is unacceptable.

When you can fully accept both sides of the story, you're free from it. Here are some truths to keep in mind:

- You're never going to be any more perfect or excellent than you are right now.
- You're not needed by anyone, ever. If you were to die, someone else would be there.
- You can't be more successful than you already are because you're a human being, and that's the most successful thing you can be.
- You can't be any more special. In fact, you're just as special and as ordinary as every other person who's ever existed, and there are billions of us.
- You will never be smart enough.
- You're not safe, and no one will save you.
- Life is boring.
- You're vulnerable and weak, the world isn't a peaceful place, and there's nothing you can do about it.

Just breathe in those sentences, and notice where you resist them. Close your eyes, and let those statements be there. Just let them be.

You're a creative energy having a human experience. When you came down here, you oriented yourself to the world and created everything we're talking about. When you can truly accept your wound, the place where you're wounded expands and becomes your superpower, while trying to fix it only makes it shrink. When you finally accept the truth, you can stop fighting it or trying to change it.

THE PROCESS

Okay, it's time. I have a process we can go through together if you're brave enough to let go. It's not a recode, it's a reset, where you go right back to the beginning and notice where all of the pain and challenges came from but don't try to change it. You just observe it and let it be.

Personal development would have you try to heal yourself and run away from it, and that's all right. But at some point, there needs to be a realization that there's this part of you that you just need to accept, and once you do, you'll become whole and live to your fullest potential. Because until you accept it, you're in denial. For example, a Type 6 accepting their wound might sound like this: "I'm really scared of being unsafe, and it freaks me out. I'm worried about where the next threat is coming from."

Once you're no longer running from your truth, it allows you to receive the power of that orientation, which is a really good thing. You see we need the Sixth superpower in the world, people who have an intuition of knowing what investments are risky, who to trust, and when to acknowledge what might go wrong. It's a superpower!

When I stopped trying to save everyone else and thought to myself, "You know what? I really love setting a big goal, going for it, working at it, and creating it. That's who I am. I'm not going to try and save people. It's not who I am."

When I allowed that to just be true and powerful, I created two hugely successful businesses with ease. You see, when you accept the wound instead of hiding from it, you go into it, claim your full superpower, and come out the other side living the fullest expression of who you are.

So you've completed the first step–becoming aware. Your consciousness is always listening, and this awareness will allow you to feel it. By acknowledging it, you're already going to be a different person.

Are you ready for the full reset?

CLAIM YOUR POWER: THE SUPERCONSCIOUS RESET EXERCISE

This process takes around thirty minutes to complete. You will need to make notes, so have a pen and paper ready, or you can use your computer or tablet.

If you would like me to take you through the process, download the free superconscious reset meditation exercise through this link https://christophermduncan.com/books/. If you would prefer to go through this on your own, find yourself a quiet space without distractions and interruptions.

PART 1: REGRESSION

1. When you're ready, close your eyes.
2. Imagine that you can revert to when you were a baby. Keep going back through the months—eleven, ten, nine, eight, seven, six, five, four, three, two, one, down through the weeks, four, three, two, one, and then the days, all the way back until you're just one day old.
3. Merge back with your mother, back in the womb. Imagine it the best you can.
4. Go back through the trimesters, third, second, and then first trimester.
5. Go all the way back, until the energy splits between your father and mother,
6. Become the universal white light before conception.

PART 2: FATHER

1. Merge consciousness with your father before the time you were conceived. Become who he was before you knew him, experiencing life the way he did
2. Now ask yourself the following questions:
    - Why might I choose this person as my father?
    - What lessons might I learn from him, good and bad?
    - What has his life been like?
    - What are his hopes, fears, ambitions, and regrets?

- How does he live life as a man?

3. When you're ready, open your eyes, and write down some notes regarding what you've acknowledged so far.

PART 3: MOTHER

1. Now, close your eyes again, and go back to the light.
2. From this perspective, merge consciousness with your mother before the time you were conceived.
3. Be the person she was before you knew her, experiencing life the way she did.
4. Now ask yourself these questions:
    - Why might I choose this person as my mother?
    - What lessons might I learn from her, good and bad?
    - What has her life been like?
    - What are her hopes, fears, ambitions, and regrets?
    - How does she live life as a woman?
5. Again, when you're ready, open your eyes, and write down some notes, connecting with the essence of your mother before you were born. What are your observations?

PART 4: PARENTS

1. When you're ready, close your eyes, return to the light, and take back with you everything you received or downloaded.
2. Ask yourself the following questions:
    - Do any of the hopes, fears, and regrets seem familiar to my life right now?
    - Are there things I avoid or have avoided?
    - Do they coincide with how I'm consciously living?
    - What's true?
3. Imagine your mother and father together, interacting at a time before you were conceived, and ask yourself these questions:
    - How does my father feel about my mother?
    - How does my mother feel about my father?
    - Are these feelings familiar in my own relationship patterns?
    - Are their interactions similar or dissimilar to how I conduct myself?
4. When you're ready, stay in the light, but open your eyes.
5. Record any observations about their energy when they're together
6. Write about why you might have chosen both of them, together, to be your parents.

PART 5: THE MOMENT OF BEING

1. When you're ready, close your eyes, and return to the light.
2. Imagine your parents making the decision, consciously, unconsciously, or even superconsciously, that they're having a child together, and that child is you.
3. Allow yourself to merge with the consciousness of your father and mother.
4. Imagine their energies coming together, and witness it like light entering a physical form. Notice what it's like when a new consciousness is born, right at the moment those two consciousnesses merge to create you.
5. Now ask yourself the following questions:
    - What are the feelings at this crucial first moment of awareness?
    - What does this consciousness feel like as it merges with them for the first time?
    - What is the spark that becomes me?
    - What's present?
    - What's the overriding feeling?
    - What is the consciousness coming from my father's side?
    - What feelings, hopes, and fears are coming through?
    - What is the consciousness coming through from my mother's side?

- What feelings, hopes, and fears are coming through?

6. Open your eyes, and then write down any observations of these two energies coming together, the masculine and the feminine, the spark of light, you, becoming something that's present.

Remember, you're connecting at that moment when the two energies came together, the clash of consciousness, that crucial moment when something is made from nothing. Then ask yourself these questions:

- Did I get a feeling of joy, abundance, scarcity, lack, obligation, pain, or hurt?
- What did I already know about myself?
- What did I already know about the family body I'm a part of?
- What did I know about my mother's body?
- Are there any feelings or knowings that are familiar from then to now?
- What was I already deciding all the way back then?

PART 6: DISCOVERY AND GROWTH

1. When you're ready, close your eyes. and return to the moment of that first spark.
2. Move forward a bit in time to when your mother was aware that she was pregnant. Remember that you're physically connected and that as a

conscious light, you're aware of your own feelings and the feelings of those around you.

3. Now ask yourself the following questions:
    - What are her feelings about this discovery?
    - How does it feel to be me being discovered?
    - What decisions am I already making?
4. Move forward to when your father is told, and ask yourself the following questions:
    - What are his feelings?
    - What am I deciding about him?
    - What am I deciding about me?
5. Now think about your feelings and decisions about the reactions and feelings of your parents, and ask yourself the following questions:
    - Has anything changed?
    - What feelings do I have toward my parents and myself?
    - Are these feelings in any way familiar to me?
6. If there's drama or trauma associated with your mother's pregnancy, ask yourself the following questions:
    - What am I deciding?
    - What's present?
    - What are my mother's feelings toward the pregnancy now that there's a problem?
    - How am I responding to the problem?
    - How does she respond?
    - What are my father's feelings about the problem?

7. Sense which of the nine orientations you may be by noticing any of these characteristics within yourself:
    - A compulsion to be perfect.
    - Needing to be needed.
    - A strong desire for success.
    - Needing to be unique.
    - An insatiable curiosity and thirst for more knowledge.
    - A yearning for security and safety.
    - A constant drive to be happy and a hunger for new experiences.
    - A desire to protect and control your environment.
    - A longing for peace at any cost.

Observe everything in your mind, noticing if there are any judgments you're receiving from either your parent or yourself.

8. When you're ready, open your eyes, and record some observations, whatever comes to you as you're going through these stages and when it starts to relate to your orientation. While you're doing this, ask yourself the following questions:
    - What am I already seeing that I can come into this world and solve or heal?
    - Do I want to fix something for my mom?
    - Do I feel the need to help my dad?

PART 7: BIRTH AND FIRST BREATH

1. Close your eyes. Return to the light at the moment of your growing, becoming, and moving toward your birth, and ask the following questions:
    - From this perspective of awareness, what are my mother's reactions and feelings during the birthing process?
    - What are my father's reactions and feelings?
    - Right in that moment when I'm coming into the world, what are my desires or fears?
    - What do I want?
    - What am I worried might happen?
    - Does anything that's happening at this moment coincide with my current life, such as when I'm facing pressure or constraints or when the spotlight is on me?
2. Imagine you're taking your first breath. Experience it now, and ask yourself these questions:
    - What information or judgments about the world are carried in my first breath?
    - What are the first words I hear?
3. As you investigate your new surroundings, becoming conscious and aware of how the world looks, ask yourself the following questions:
    - Do I feel safe?
    - Do I feel unsafe?
    - Does this feel like a place I want to conquer?
    - Is this a terrifying place to hide from?

- Is this a flawed place that needs to be perfected?
- Is this a wounded place that needs to be helped?
- Is this a place where I could have fun?
- What rules am I creating?

4. You see your mother for the first time. Ask yourself the following questions:
    - What are my feelings toward her?
    - What are my feelings toward the feminine?
    - How do I react?
    - How does she react?
5. Notice the energy of your father, and ask yourself the following questions:
    - Is he there?
    - How do I react to the masculine being there or not?
    - Do I feel the need to fix, heal, prove, or please?
    - Do these thoughts and feelings seem in any way familiar to me as I am now when meeting new people or in unfamiliar situations?
6. Open your eyes, and write down your thoughts.

PART 8: INDEPENDENCE

1. When you're ready, you can close your eyes and return to the moment the cord is cut that ties you to the mother.

2. This is your first time being an independent being. You still rely on others, but you're now able to operate with autonomy and express yourself. Ask yourself these questions about being separated:
    - How do I feel?
    - Do I have a longing to reconnect?
    - Am I happy about it?
    - What's my first thought?
    - What's my first action?
    - What are my conscious or unconscious judgments?
    - Do I have any self-judgment?
    - What pain do I see around my parents?
    - Are my needs immediately being met, and by whom?
    - Am I given nourishment?
    - How does it feel to be given nourishment or not?
    - If I do receive nourishment, do I feel guilty about receiving it?
    - Do I feel happy about it?
3. At this point, you might make a contract with your parents. If so, ask yourself these questions:
    - What can I solve for them?
    - Do I need to be an example?
    - Do I need to be a helper?
    - Do I tell my mom I love her, and that I promise to be good?

- Do I tell my dad that I love him, and I promise to listen to him?
- How will I honor these contracts?
- Do I also enter into a contract with the world to make it a better place?

4. When you're ready, you can open your eyes and record as much as you like. Just write all that down.

WHAT DID YOU LEARN?

1. Close your eyes, and ask yourself these questions:
    - From the perspective of the adult who just went on that epic journey again, what is the overriding feeling or mood of the unconscious?
    - What is it trying to do for itself or others?
    - What is the wound?
    - Where does it see itself or others are lacking?
    - What is its compensating strategy?
    - After everything I've learned so far, what do I think my unconscious believes life is about?
    - What do I sense about my unconsciousness in relationships?
    - How does my unconscious react to freedom or happiness?

2. Open your eyes, and write this all down. Just let it all out, and figure out what you learned from the experience

THE AFTERMATH

You've just pushed the button on a huge change in your consciousness, begun the process of healing the wound, and activated your superconscious superpower.

How do you feel?

The truth with this exercise is that it's profound. Things change at a fundamental level that you've believed, feared, and fought against your whole life long are being accepted and integrated into your being. And because it's so profound, so deep, so central to your identity, you need to go through the process more than once.

Over the next week or two, it's important to revisit this and sit with your wound again and again, until you no longer have a desire to change it and just accept that it's true. I know it's difficult, but if you do this once a day for nine days, you will become so aware of the wound that it will no longer be something you're scared of. I guarantee it.

You'll go back and acknowledge some truths and write them down so the next time you go back and do the exercise, you'll sit with it, and this is the key, not try to change it. Just ask yourself, "Why would I choose this?" and an answer will come to you. The more you sit with it and meditate on it, the less it's a problem, until it's not a problem. At some point, your system will send the message, "Okay, yes, it happened."

If you want to take it further, you can move forward to age one, age two, and so on, asking yourself what it was like, how it felt, and what was going on. It's already a repeating pattern. Go through the next phase, and let this unfold. And as it does, don't try to change it. Just let it be. The more you try to fix it, run from it, or create a life to get away from it, the more it follows you around. You know this because you've lived it.

But if you go back, sift through everything, acknowledge it all, and then sit with the truth, it will be integrated. Yes, it will hurt, but it will be okay. When you truly find the places where the pain is, the key is to accept it because your shadow is you, and the more you let it in, the more you receive your superpower.

You'll realize that everything you thought was harming you was your superconscious nudging you to create your superpower. All of a sudden, you'll understand that everything you thought was against you, was for you, and all of your pain was the mold that created your higher self, helping you discover people, places, and situations, in a superconsciously designed system, to create a very specific superconscious power.

BECOMING SUPERCONSCIOUS

After you've done the reset exercise for nine days, you'll start to feel profound shifts in your life, which means it's time to fully integrate your shadow. To help you reach this goal, I have a meditation that's focused on giving up trying to fix the wound and instead receiving your full superpower. There's a video where I guide you through it that you can access *here*. But if you want to do it on your own, I've provided it below

As you go into the healing meditation, remember that the low side is just a shadow of the high side. They're the same person, it's just that one is dysfunctional and the other is a genius accessing their superpower.

In summary, you'll do this meditation nine times, as if you're each type. I recommend referring to the orientation outlines provided in chapters five to thirteen.

MEDITATION

All types should do this meditation nine times, substituting the consecutive type for each one–for instance, "Step into the Type 1 dysfunction," "Step into the Type 2 dysfunction," etc.–until you get through all nine.

PART 1

1. When you're ready, close your eyes, and as you do, allow yourself to receive a feeling of innocence.
2. Take yourself on a familiar path down into a forest and out into a meadow filled with beautiful purple flowers, and into a spiritual building that reaches up to the night sky.
3. Connect with your innocence again just for a moment, giving up the need to know what's out there.
4. Step into the type (1–9) dysfunction and say to yourself, "Superconscious, show me a symbol or a person who will guide me."
5. Ask your superconscious to give you information about what it's like to be a dysfunctional type (1 through 9).
6. Completely embody the type (1–9) dysfunctional traits, where you have their fears, and just feel what it's like to sit in their orientation.
7. Open your eyes, and make some notes about what's it like to be at the dysfunctional level of the type (1–9).
8. Sit with this for a while.

PART 2

1. Close your eyes again, and step back into that exact same experience.

2. Make peace with your internal war. Accept all parts of yourself and of the world around you, and allow yourself to receive the gift of the type (1–9).
3. Now allow yourself to rise right to the top of the type (1–9) orientation, where you shift into your best self.
4. Just breathe that in, and sit with it for a second, noticing what it's like to be in this phase. What's life like when you're here? What's it like when you've risen to the top and you've let go of all of the fears?
5. Observe what's obvious and what's true about rising to the highest level of the type (1–9). How does it feel? What's life about when you're here?
6. Open your eyes, and write down what you learned. Then sit with it.

CHAPTER 15

LESSONS LEARNED: A REVIEW

YOUR TRUE NATURE

- You're not just blood, flesh, and bone; you're a creative energy having a human experience.
- Your consciousness has three elements–the self-conscious chooses and decides where you're going in life, the unconscious either allows it to happen or not, and the superconscious comes up with ways to turn the dream into reality.
- For most people, these three parts don't work well together because the unconscious wants survival, and the self-conscious wants the good life, which puts them in conflict.

- To experience this life, you descend into a singular perspective and enter a limited vehicle, your body, that orients you to the world.
- You learn that you're just a vulnerable baby and inadequate to survive here. This learning creates a wound that's so painful and scary that you must never accept it as true.
- Because the pain is unacceptable, you create a strategy that allows you to escape it. This compensating strategy is created in two different minds:

    1. Your unconscious creates an agenda that won't allow the pain to be true by creating a life designed to avoid it.
    2. Your superconscious creates a superpower that gives access to intuitive wisdom.

- Your unconscious is a pattern of what it's learned is safe. Anything else is a threat. Its main objective is ensuring you survive, and the resulting desire to keep things as they are is called the unconscious agenda.
- The self-conscious seeks change and wants to thrive.
- This conflict between the unconscious and self-conscious leads to a life of oscillation, with lots of desire and action, but never really getting anywhere.

YOUR LIFE FOCUS

- There are effectively two ways to be focused in life: solving a problem or creating a new reality.
- To create real change and achieve big results, you need to learn how to live in a creative-oriented life structure instead of a problem-oriented one.
- You either try to escape the wound or live in a desired reality.
- You're either creating magic or trying to avoid the truthfulness of your wound.
- Your superpower lies dormant, waiting for you to let go of the wound and activate it. Until you do, you're just living in the shadow of your life.

CHAPTER 16

WHAT'S NEXT?

You've learned a lot during the course of this book, such as

- how you live in your shadow rather than in your true light;
- the trinity of the consciousness (the self-conscious, the unconscious, and the superconscious) and how your childhood wound is used by the unconscious to keep you alive and in a trap;
- the two structures in life, the problem orientation and the creative orientation, and how the first keeps you stuck while the second helps you get into flow; and
- the ancient wisdom of the Enneagram and the nine orientations.

You've been given the missing piece of the puzzle, the lost learning about how your wound can become your superconscious superpower, and completed the first step of the superconscious reset process.

NEXT STEPS

If you're ready to really take your life to the next level, I would highly recommend joining me or one of my coaches at one of our superconscious upgrade live experiences. You can find out more information on our website.

ABOUT THE AUTHOR

Christopher M. Duncan is a New Zealander who lives in the Gold Coast, Australia, with his wife, Harriet. After a near-death experience in 2009, he dedicated his life to understanding how to create success and find meaning in the laws of the universe.

What he discovered was that most people have been misled about the fundamental ways in which manifestation really works. After studying one-on-one with some of the most transformational minds in the world, Christopher created the Magnetic Mind Method, teaching others how to become superconscious and create anything they desire.

Printed in Great Britain
by Amazon

50075872R00136